TOMATOES
ARE SPIRITUAL TOO

FRUIT OR VEGETABLE?

Gregg L. Marshall

TOMATOES ARE SPIRITUAL TOO

DEDICATION

To my tomato-loving children:

Kimberlyn and Jeremiah

Reviews

*"I have been honored and deeply humbled as I have had the privilege of reading your manuscript before publishing. Thank you so very much! This book is simple and easy to read, full of great quotes, Scriptures, stories, and personal experiences. I have thoroughly enjoyed reading your book. In addition to teaching the main topic, there were many other very valuable lessons to be learned for a Christian to overcome pain, problems, and persecution. (I like alliteration too!) The questions at the end of the chapters were very thought-provoking. I would definitely recommend this book to every Christian. I would encourage others to use this book as a teaching tool." ~ **Terri Jo Moyer, proofreader**

*"This is not your typical garden variety book. Who would have thought there were so many spiritual lessons contained within the ever-popular tomato? Is it a fruit or a vegetable? What can be learned from the unique space it occupies between the two food groups? It was all beyond me until I read Pastor Gregg Marshall's engaging tribute to the tomato. Full of spiritual insights and encouragements, this book will capture your imagination from the start and hold your attention as the pages turn. For those who allow its lessons to penetrate their hearts, a closer walk with Jesus will be the result." ~ **Pastor David Huston, Carlisle, PA**

*"It has been a joy and an honor to be involved in the preparation process of this book. It has challenged me in more ways than one. It has caused me to look at things in a different light. I enjoyed the questions at the end of each chapter because they provoke you to retain the information you have read while also getting your perspective. I would recommend any Christian, on any level of spiritual maturity, to read this book as it is easy to read and deeply challenging at the same time." ~ **Rachael E. Kellett, proofreader**

"I thoroughly enjoyed reading this book! It is well-written and easy to understand. The stories are funny yet have depth to them. This book is very thought-provoking and is backed up with Scripture. It doesn't just hit one topic, but many all wrapping up together. Being part of this process has been an honor and a humbling privilege. I have never done anything like this before. God has truly blessed this project, and we can see that He was completely in control during the writing of this book!"
~ **Valerie Zellers, proofreader**

CONTENTS

Introduction

Why The Tomato?

"Gardening is cheaper than therapy, and you get tomatoes."
~ Author Unknown

The tomato is one of life's complex mysteries and is surrounded by much controversy. That may sound humorous, even absurd, but the question "Is the tomato a fruit or a vegetable?" was taken as far as the United States Supreme Court. To this day, countless people are confused about this. When they find out the truth of the matter, many are baffled, and some choose to remain in denial.

Why does it matter if the tomato is a fruit or a vegetable?

 Who cares? As odd as it sounds, we can learn biblical principles from a simple, plump, juicy tomato. Understanding its placement in the proper category unlocks insightful truths about what has been imparted to us and what is intended for Christians to exemplify in their day-to-day lives.

Suppose you enjoy tomatoes as much as my two oldest children (to whom this book is dedicated). They eat them often and will eat them raw in any shape or size, especially picked fresh from our home garden. It amazes my wife and I when they want to eat tomatoes without seasoning or being accompanied by something else. They just want to eat tomatoes; they would eat a tomato like you would an apple if we would give them the opportunity. My wife and I have never enjoyed tomatoes like our children.

You may not enjoy tomatoes like our kids, who will grab their fistfuls and pile them on their dinner plates. Maybe you are a little more like my wife and I, who prefer them in salads, sandwiches, and spaghetti sauce. Perhaps you don't like tomatoes at all, but you are curious about what this book contains. *My goal is that you will never look at tomatoes the same way again, and every time you see a tomato, this book and its contents will come to your remembrance.* I pray that you will be forever impacted, that the biblical principles within these pages will transform your mind, and that you will find the necessary tools to live them out.

The subject of this book (soon to be revealed) has well been forgotten and even blatantly forsaken by many modern Christians. The contents of these pages will likely be challenging and thought-provoking. I have attempted to write this book in a down-to-earth, light-hearted, and engaging fashion. If you have ever smelled **rotting tomatoes**,  you will agree with the following statement: we don't need another book with stale, moldy, decaying religious discourses without spiritual application, practicality, and demonstration.

May the pages of this little book bring you a light-hearted, attainable, and insightful appreciation for the biblical principles and applications of the spiritual truths surrounding the tomato. It has been fashioned as if we are in an intimate home or Small Group Bible Study, where connection, laughter, a little sarcasm, storytelling, and interaction are intended. At the end of each chapter, you will find questions to "make it personal."

So, before we "dive in," I welcome you to go to the kitchen and prepare a serving of fresh tomatoes or make a fresh tomato sandwich (they are best with mayo, salt, and pepper). Be sure to grab your favorite drink as we prepare for an engaging and enlightening spiritual journey.

Chapter 1

TOMATO: A Fruit Or A Vegetable?

"Give a man a fish, he eats for a day.
Teach a man to garden and the whole neighborhood gets tomatoes."
~ Pinterest

According to the Dictionary, the tomato is defined as "*any of several plants belonging to the genus Lycopersicon, of the nightshade family, native to Mexico and Central and South America, bearing a mildly acid, pulpy, usually red fruit eaten raw or cooked as a vegetable, the fruit itself.*" [1]

The Oxford Learner's Dictionary defines tomato as "*a soft fruit with a lot of juice and shiny red skin that is eaten as a vegetable either raw or cooked.*" [2]

The Cambridge Dictionary defines a tomato as a "*round, red fruit with a lot of seeds, eaten cooked or uncooked as a vegetable, for example in salads or sauces.*" [3]

Do you see the confusion? All three above sources claim that the tomato is a fruit but is eaten or cooked as a vegetable.

Like myself, many of us can only shake our heads and say, "What?" How can something that belongs in my vegetable salad be a fruit? How can my spaghetti, lasagna, and pizza sauce be made from a fruit? I have never had tomatoes served with a fruit salad!! The very thought of it turns my stomach.

This whole thing is messed up; something has gone terribly wrong here. In our minds, putting watermelons and tomatoes in the same food group may be absurd. Honestly, a tomato does not even taste remotely like fruit compared to an apple, peach, or banana (or any other fruit, for that matter).

Believe it or not, this overly complicated question and debate found its way to the United States Supreme Court in 1893. Apparently, when you  cannot figure something out, and it is this complex ... get the government involved! They can clear it up and make things less complicated, right? WRONG! The Supreme Court ruled that while the tomato is **a fruit**, it is also **a vegetable**. Wow! That helped!

According to Wikipedia, *Nix v. Hedden*, 149 U.S. 304 (1893), was a decision by the Supreme Court of the United States that, under U.S. customs regulations, the tomato should be classified as a vegetable rather than a fruit. The Court's unanimous opinion held that the Tariff Act of 1883 used the ordinary meaning of "fruit" and "vegetable" instead of the technical botanical sense.

John Nix founded the John Nix & Co. Fruit Commission in New York City in 1839. The company became one of the largest produce sellers in New York City at the time and was one of the first to ship produce from Virginia, Florida, and Bermuda to New York.

In 1883, President Chester A. Arthur signed the Tariff Act of March 3, 1883, requiring a tax to be paid on imported vegetables, but not fruits. The John Nix & Co. filed a suit against Edward L. Hedden, Collector of the Port of New York, to recover back duties paid under protest. They argued against the tariff by pointing out that, botanically, a tomato is a fruit due to its seed-bearing structure growing from the flowering part of a plant.

The Court unanimously decided in favor of the respondent and found that the tomato should classify, under the customs regulations, as **a vegetable** based on how the public uses it. Justice Horace Gray wrote the opinion for the Court, stating that:

"The passages cited from the dictionaries define the word 'fruit' as the seed of plants, or that part of plants which contains the seed, and especially the juicy, pulpy products of certain plants, covering and containing the seed. These definitions do not tend to show that tomatoes are 'fruit,' as distinguished from 'vegetables,' in common speech, or within the meaning of the tariff act."

Justice Gray acknowledged that botanically, tomatoes are classified as a **"fruit of the vine"**; however, they are seen as vegetables because they were usually eaten as a main course instead of eaten as a dessert. [4]

Now, that just cleared everything up for us, didn't it? *Not at all!* Many people today are still just as confused about this whole issue. In fact, American states are conflicted about this, and it is comical.

Tomatoes are the state vegetable of New Jersey and Louisiana (creole tomato). Tomatoes are the official state fruit of Ohio and Tennessee. Arkansas was brilliant; they covered both sides of the argument. In Arkansas, the South Arkansas Vine Ripe Pink Tomato is both the states official fruit and the State's official vegetable! [5]

In a nutshell, here is the whole thing: because it functions as the ovary of a flowering plant, a tomato is naturally (botanically) a **fruit**. But many people do not associate it as such because of its taste, which is less sweet than others, like mangos, kiwis, oranges, etc. Now add to that: people culturally use tomatoes with other vegetables when cooking and serving "non-dessert" items.

So, let us address the "elephant in the room." I know most of us are wondering, **what right does THIS GUY have to be one of the leading characters on "Veggie Tales?"** Why is a fruit a central character on a show with a bunch of vegetables? Confusion abounds! We are all asking, "What about Bob?"

I understand if you need to take a few moments to process all this. I had to process it, too. For most of my life, I was under the impression that a tomato was a vegetable, like "duh"! It was a ridiculous notion to consider it as anything else. Yet, here we are, talking about it! The reality is that although the tomato is classified, eaten, served, and culturally accepted and recognized as a vegetable, *scientifically* (or botanically) it is a fruit.

I will not dive into specifics because I am not addressing biblical doctrines in this book. Still, one must honestly ask, "Has the church classified matters as one thing while the Bible identifies them as something else?" Do we, as the church, culturally and unquestioningly accept ceremonies and rituals merely because they have been "traditionally accepted" for centuries? Have we honestly asked ourselves, "What does the **Bible** say about the practices and procedures in my local assembly?"

As we see in the case of the tomato, we can culturally accept something and classify it as something that it is genuinely not. As Christians, we must always be interested in TRUTH! Because the truth liberates, purifies, sanctifies, and sets us apart for God's intended use. *"Sanctify them by Your truth. Your word is truth"* (John 17:17).

Words and actions have immense power and influence. They can deflect or direct. Let us ever be in pursuit of the liberating power of truth! Truth always liberates, while lies and deception break down, distract, destroy, and deeply scar.

Lori Carrell once said, "When a friend describes a beautiful sunset, a picture is created in our mind. The words enable you to make meaning. When a parent reacts to a child's artwork, meaning is created between child and parent, which can affect the child's self-concept for a lifetime.

"Likewise, when a lie is spoken, a false reality is constructed that, once discovered, can rupture relationships. For example, when Bill Clinton's inner circle believed his lie that he hadn't had relations with Monica Lewinsky, their minds accepted an 'unreal reality.' Their eventual discovery of the truth and resulting feelings of betrayal were probably more dramatic than those who hadn't believed Clinton in the first place. This power to affect one another is serious business. Our spoken words shape the reality of those with whom we interact." [6]

We must understand that if we want to see God's will and works accomplished in our lives and spheres of influence, we must have an acute interest in the truth.

"For the word of the Lord is right, and all His work is done in truth" (Psalm 33:4). If we sincerely desire to be partnered with God, His Word, and His works, we must be connected and in constant cadence with biblical truth.

Though it is culturally accepted and even classified (by very influential entities and people) as a vegetable, the hard scientific truth is **the tomato is a fruit!** It has been established. As we slowly move beyond the wrestling match of this reality, we begin to see that other juicy and savory truths begin to emerge.

MAKE IT PERSONAL

✦━━━━━━━━━━━━•━━━━━━━━━━━━•✦

1.) Before you read this chapter, what did you classify the tomato as, a fruit or a vegetable? Explain why.

_____

_____

_____

_____

2.) What are some things society generally classifies as acceptable behavior but the Bible clearly states as unacceptable?

_____

_____

_____

_____

3.) Has the church accepted non-biblical practices, rituals, and ceremonies which cannot be found in Scripture? Or, have they disregarded biblical practices as "no longer available for us to experience in our day?" (See Mark 16:15-18, John 14:11-13, Acts 2:37-43, and Hebrews 13:8.)

_____

_____

_____

_____

"Mountaintops are for views
and inspiration, but fruit is
grown in the valleys."

~ Billy Graham

Chapter 2

What Is the "Tomato" Of The Spirit?

"Knowledge is knowing that a tomato is a fruit. Wisdom is not putting it in a fruit salad." ~ Miles Kington

After my intensive, rigorous, and exhaustive research on the tomato (a whole 54 minutes), this made me wonder, "If the tomato is a fruit, then what is the 'tomato' of the fruit of the Spirit?" I imagined God handing me a fruit basket with perfectly ripe apples, bananas, oranges, mangos, and kiwis, and right in the middle of this display … there is … a tomato! "What!?" That is interesting, admittedly weird, but immensely powerful.

Suppose the tomato is culturally associated more with a vegetable because of its lack of sweetness, more so than other fruits. Does it make it any less of a fruit? Surely not! So, what fruit of the Spirit would represent a tomato? In a basket full of other, much sweeter fruits, which of the "fruit of the Spirit" would be represented by a plump, juicy, less sweet tomato?

What Is The Tomato Of The Spirit?

"But the fruit of the Spirit is love, joy, peace, longsuffering, gentleness, goodness, faith, meekness, temperance: against such there is no law" (Galatians 5:22-23 KJV).

A BRIEF LOOK INTO THE FRUIT BASKET

Is **LOVE** a sweet fruit? The Greek word in this passage is *agape*. It is found 116 times in the Bible. It is translated as "*affection or benevolence, specifically, a love feast.*" It comes from the Greek word, which indicates "*much love.*" Ask the parentless child, a grieving widow, or an abused individual what they long for most. Obviously, we can agree that love would classify as a "sweet fruit" of the Spirit on every occasion.

Richard Paul Evans reiterated, "I once heard it said that everyone needs love – and if they're denied, they'll find it or a reasonable substitute somewhere." No one should ever need to look for a substitute. *"Beloved, let us love one another, for love is of God; and everyone who loves is born of God and knows God. He who does not love does not know God, for God is love"* (1 John 4:7-8).

Is **JOY** a sweet fruit? The Greek word is *chara*. It is found 59 times in the Bible and translated as "*cheerfulness, a calm delight.*" It comes from the Greek word, which indicates "*full of cheer and exceedingly.*" Ask those overwhelmed by depression, anxiety, and fear if an experience of joy would bring a sweet refreshing to their minds, emotions, and bodies.

In 2017, the World Health Organization reported that depression is the leading cause of disability worldwide and significantly contributes to the overall global burden of disease. The National Institute of Mental Health revealed that neuropsychiatric disorders are the leading cause of disability in the U.S., with *major depressive disorder* being the most common. [7]

The Employee Assistance Professionals Association Survey 2017 stated that mental health (depression, grief, and behavioral conduct) is the second leading workplace concern, following only family issues.

Some sources say that every year, depression costs an estimated $100 billion for U.S. employers, which includes $44 billion in lost productivity alone. [8] We clearly see that we need a revival of joy because it is a "sweet fruit" of the Spirit.

Is **PEACE** a sweet fruit? The Greek word is *eirēnē*. It is found 92 times in the Bible, and it comes from the primary verb meaning *"to join."* It is translated as *"peace (literally or figuratively), prosperity, rest, and quietness."* We can easily classify peace as a "sweet fruit" of the Spirit to those pressing and stretching themselves to their maximum potential and those struggling to attain theirs. Ask the new business owner working 80 hours a week or the single mother of three children if they would appreciate the soothing caress of the sweet fruit of peace in their life.

Is **GENTLENESS** a sweet fruit? The Greek word is *chrēstotēs*. It is found only 10 times in the Bible and translated as *"usefulness, moral excellence (in character and demeanor)."* It comes from the Greek meaning *"useful in manner or morals,* *gracious and kind.*" Ask the struggling business owner looking for amicable, trustworthy, and dependable representatives. We can undoubtedly classify gentleness as a "sweet fruit" of the Spirit in stressful, compromising, or depleted times.

Is **FAITH** a sweet fruit? The Greek word is *pistis*. It is found 244 times in the Bible and comes from the Greek word meaning *"convinced and persuaded."* It is translated as *"persuasion, moral conviction, a reliance (upon Christ), consistency, assurance, and fidelity."*

We live in a generation that consistently uproots itself and wanders from place to place. They have everywhere to go but no place to stay. It is becoming more challenging to keep track of some people. Ask any number of pastors, employers, friends, and family members if they would welcome moral convictions, reliance, consistency, and fidelity.

According to the United States Census Bureau, "Using 2007 ACS data, it is estimated that a person in the United States can expect to move 11.7 times in their lifetime

based upon the current age structure and average rates and allowing for no more than one move per single year. At age 18, a person can expect to move another 9.1 times in their remaining lifetime, but by age 45, the expected number of moves is only 2.7." [9] Given these statistics, we can indeed classify faith (or faithfulness) as a "sweet fruit" of the Spirit that is essential in this wandering generation.

Is **MEEKNESS** a sweet fruit? The Greek word is *praotēs*. It is found only nine times in the Bible and translated as "*a humility that is gentle.*" Synonymous terms are submissive, obedient, unassuming, and courteous. We can absolutely classify meekness as a "sweet fruit" of the Spirit, especially when we have lost our way and need direction and help.

Take a moment to recall how relieved you felt when you were lost in a large department store, auditorium, or airport and you needed to seek out an employee or the Customer Courtesy Desk. Or, how grateful you were when Triple A showed up when your automobile was unmovable on a back road in the middle of the night. Have you ever had such moments of stress and pressure? If so, you will agree that the sweetness of these courteous moments in high-stress situations is greatly appreciated.

Is **TEMPERANCE** a sweet fruit? The Greek word is *egkrateia*. It is found only four times in the Bible and translates as "*self-control, continence, and restraint.*" It comes from the Greek word meaning "*masterful in controlling self and its appetites, to be strong.*" Admittedly, this fruit may not be as sweet as the others we have discussed, but it is sweet at its center.

Ask the Plant Manager dealing with a crisis on the production floor if he would appreciate staff members with level heads and patience compared to panic, anxiety, fear, or self-preservation. Some may never experience a job site crisis, but many have experienced the daunting task of grocery shopping with an infant or toddler.

The story is told about a man who stopped in the grocery store on the way home from work to pick up a couple of items for his wife. He wandered around aimlessly for a while, searching out the needed groceries. As is often the case in the grocery store, he passed this same shopper in nearly every aisle. It was another father trying to shop with an uncooperative three-year-old boy in the cart.

The first time they passed, the three-year-old repeatedly asked (more accurately, whined) for a piece of candy. The observing shopper could not hear the entire

conversation. He just overheard the dad say, "Now, Johnny, this won't take long." As they passed in the next aisle, the three-year-old's pleas had increased by several octaves. Now the dad was quietly saying, "Johnny, just calm down. We will be done in a minute." When they passed near the dairy section, the boy was screaming uncontrollably.

The dad was keeping his cool. In an incredibly low voice, he said, "Johnny, settle down. We are almost out of here." The dad and his son reached the checkout counter just ahead of the observer. He still gave no evidence of losing control. The boy was screaming and kicking. The dad was very calm, saying over and over, "Johnny, we will be in the car in just a minute, and then everything will be OK."

The bystander was impressed beyond words. After paying for his groceries, he hurried to catch up with this father, who was a fantastic example of patience and self-control, just in time to hear him say again, "Johnny, we're done. It's going to be OK." He tapped the patient father on the shoulder and said, "Sir, I couldn't help but watch how you handled little Johnny. You were amazing." The dad replied, "You don't get it, do you?" *I'm Johnny!"*

While that is very humorous, I am sure it was not funny at the time for this frustrated father. But in a situation such as this, or in moments of crisis, we can undoubtedly classify temperance as a "sweet fruit" of the Spirit. Though it may not be as sweet as the others, those who witness this fruit in action taste its sweetness and sincerely appreciate and admire it.

Lastly, is **LONGSUFFERING** a sweet fruit? The Greek word is *makrothumia*, translated as *"longanimity, forbearance, patience, fortitude, and an enduring temper."* The first word, "longanimity," is not used in modern terminology but means *"a disposition to bear injuries long and with patience."*

Longsuffering is found 17 times in the Word of God. There are only four verses in the Old Testament, and each time it is used, it means the same thing. It comes from two Hebrew words. The first means *"to tarry, slow to do"* and the second pictures *"a nose on a face, in wrath or intense anger."* It paints a vivid picture of rapid breathing through the nose in anger. (Have you ever been there or put anyone in that position?) When we put the two words together, it means "slow to make very angry."

Many have given the simple yet accurate definition of longsuffering as "to suffer long." Nothing about the word sounds appealing to this drive-thru, frozen dinner, instant mashed potato, "Have it YOUR Way," "If it feels good, do it," "Looking out for #1," "My way or the highway," generation!

For those who are not the most patient (myself included), polished, or persevering, longsuffering does NOT look or even taste appealing or sweet compared to all the other fruits in the basket! But Jesus thought it necessary that it be in there.

I think we have finally identified the "tomato of the Spirit." It is still a fruit but tastes less sweet than the others. It seems to be in a whole other category than the sweeter fruits. But God included it in the fruit basket, and *"against such there is no law"* (Galatians 5:23).

The Apostle Paul saw a tomato in his fruit basket, looked it over, and said, *"I want to know Christ and experience the mighty power that raised him from the dead. I want to suffer with him, sharing in his death, so that one way or another I will experience the resurrection from the dead"* (Philippians 3:10-11 NLT).

Suffering? Really? Is this book about suffering? You are half right; this book is about **long**-suffering.

Life is full of pains, pressures, and problems. And God has equipped us with a fruit basket for the journey. You have two choices right now: first, you can close the book and handle your situations and circumstances as best you can, in your human understanding. Or, second, you can agree that God has placed a plump, juicy tomato in your fruit basket. *See, tomatoes are spiritual, too!* He wants you to understand what Longsuffering is so you can be empowered with the spiritual tools to be an overcomer.

If we are to be "Christians" or "Christ-like," we will all have to endure some degree of suffering. But Jesus is Emmanuel, "God with us" through it all. If the God of this universe came to earth, manifesting Himself as the "suffering servant," who do we think we are to expect an exemption card from suffering?

In her book *Glorious Weakness: Discovering God in All We Lack*, Alia Joy shares a powerful testimony:

"In the summer of 2012, I knelt over the frail shell of a child, my son, strapped to all manner of medical monitoring equipment. His body failing, his frame thinning, the medical staff at Arkansas Children's Hospital was at a loss. They had no answers, no direction. He was an anomaly, they said, and they'd need to regroup after making him as comfortable as possible. Though the medical community struggled to sort it all out, my faith community seemed to have every answer.

"God would provide, one said, because God would respond to my great faith. God was setting up a miracle, another said. God works all things together for good, I was reminded. Platitude, platitude, platitude. I smiled through all of them, even nodded. Silently I wondered, did all those words amount to anything, well-meaning though they were? Hunched over my son, all those platitudes haunting, my phone rang.

"I looked at the screen, read the name. It was a pastor from a more reformed church in my hometown, and as I answered the phone, I wondered what platitude I might hear. There was a purpose in my son's suffering? Everything has a Kingdom purpose? After an exchange of greetings, I clenched my jaw. Stiffened. Braced myself.

"Through the phone, I heard only three words: "I'm so sorry." There was a pause, and he told me to holler if I needed anything. He said he'd be praying, and that was that. It was a moment of selfless solidarity, a moment in which this man of the cloth didn't force-feed me anemic answers or sell me some fix-all version of a bright-and-shiny gospel.

"Instead, he did the work of Christ himself; he entered into my suffering. And years later, after a long season of healing (both my son's and my own), his words served as a reminder of the Christian response to suffering—we enter into it together, share in it together, lament with each other.

"I suppose it's natural, our tendency to try to run from suffering, to somehow try to drag other folks from their own. We Christians use the holy tools at our disposal (particularly, the misinterpretation of Scripture) in an attempt to pave a path around suffering. The problem is that's not the way of Christ. Christ—God with us—entered into the suffering of humanity. He lamented with those who lamented, extended compassion and healing to the hurting. Ultimately, he took on the existential suffering of all mankind as he endured his own suffering on the cross." [10]

Though we have not asked for the adverse, it proves to us that the Word of God is true, as it declares that *"The steps of a good man are ordered* (established) *by the Lord, and He delights in his way"* (Psalm 37:23).

It is a natural tendency to run away and avoid suffering at all costs; after all, who would choose to suffer?  Some would try to focus all their energy, attention, and presentations on spiritual victories and elevations, altogether avoiding the daily struggles of life. Often, these daily struggles take more than a week, a month, or even a year to overcome. The reality is that we cannot experience a triumph without overcoming opposition. We will not be elevated to higher spiritual dimensions until we have first conquered our current dimension of living.

God has ordered and established your steps, and if you are currently facing a fierce, prolonged, tumultuous storm, be encouraged. The prophet Nahum declared, *"The Lord is slow to anger and great in power, and will not at all acquit the wicked. The Lord has His way in the whirlwind and in the storm, and the clouds are the dust of His feet. The Lord is good, a stronghold in the day of trouble; and He knows those who trust in Him"* (Nahum 1:3,7).

We naturally want to run and find shelter from storms. But we find, in Matthew 14:22, that *"Immediately Jesus made His disciples get into the boat and go before Him to the other side, while He sent the multitudes away."* Jesus knew a storm was coming, yet he *"made His disciples get into the boat."* There are personal, God-ordained storms that we must go through that the multitudes will never witness. But rest assured that if you  continue to walk in His path, the miraculous will show up somewhere!

Suppose God orders our steps, and we find ourselves going headlong into storms and contrary winds. In that case, this proves that we need to have a proper and biblical understanding of the spiritual fruit called **longsuffering**. Yes, it doesn't taste nearly as sweet as the other fruits in our basket, but it has been given to us nonetheless.

Our elders admit that their far-reaching anointing, skills, impact, and influence were all forged in times of intense, prolonged testing and trials. None of it would be possible if they didn't endure the long hours of constant pressure. Compare it to the wonderful taste of a homemade soup that has simmered for hours. Homemade soup is my favorite because it is much fresher, more anticipated, appreciated, and savored when all the flavors and seasonings have had time to spread throughout the pot. Nothing compares to the house's aroma as you walk in the door on a cold, damp day.

So it is in this life that we will experience the cooking pot (or crockpot) of prolonged heat and pressure;  the Bible calls them "fiery trials." But when our victory finally is achieved, we will be able to serve our generation with something so much more satisfying and savory than a cheap Campbell's Condensed Soup ever could. Are you "the real deal," or are you merely equipped with regurgitated talking points? People can smell (sense) if you are a "crockpot" or a "condensed" kind of person.

We will *taste and see that the Lord is good*" (Psalm 34:8). In the following chapters, we will start unpacking some practical, life-changing principles God has intended for us to discover in His Word about the tomato of the Spirit. Let's continue on our journey. I'm excited to take this journey with you.

MAKE IT PERSONAL

1.) What does the thought of longsuffering or "suffering long" do to your mind, emotions, and spirit? Does it bring anxiety, fear, or confident faith?

_____

_____

_____

_____

2.) What purposes do you think God has in giving us the tomato of longsuffering?

_____

_____

_____

_____

3.) Several Scriptures were given in this chapter regarding suffering, pressure, and storms; what did these Scriptures challenge you to think or encounter?

_____

_____

_____

_____

A mother once approached Napoleon seeking a pardon for her son. The emperor replied that the young man had committed a certain offense twice and justice demanded death.

"But I don't ask for justice,? the mother explained. "I plead for *mercy*!"

"But your son does not deserve *mercy*," Napoleon replied.

"Sir," the woman cried, "it would not be *mercy* if he deserved it, and *mercy* is all I ask for."

"Well, then," the emperor said, "I will have *mercy*."

And he spared the woman's son.

Luis Palau, Experiencing God's Forgiveness, Multnomah Press, 1984

Chapter 3

.•——————•——————•.

Teamed Up With Mercy

"A world without tomatoes is like a string quartet without violins."

~ Laura Colwin

Longsuffering is a product of God's love toward us. I am so thankful that God "puts up" with our antics, attitudes, and apathies. We should be exceedingly grateful that our God is slow to anger. The Psalmist revealed, *"The LORD is merciful and gracious, slow to anger, and abounding in mercy"* (Psalm 103:8).

It is incredible to know that God **chooses** to be merciful and gracious to us. What's more, He doesn't give it hesitantly or reservedly. The Scripture says He is *"abounding in mercy"* (Psalm 103:8). The prophet Micah declared that God *"delights in mercy"* (Micah 7:18). This very truth is the only reason why many of us are still alive today and have the privilege to serve the Lord. Our lives would look drastically different if it weren't for His mercy. Without God's mercies, where would we be?

If we simply looked up Scriptures with the word "longsuffering," we would see a pattern emerge. It is a pattern that speaks volumes about the nature of God. We would quickly see that longsuffering is teamed up with mercy. Laying hold on this truth alone should cause us to pause and be sincerely thankful.

"And the Lord passed before him and proclaimed, 'The Lord, the

Lord God, merciful and gracious, longsuffering, and abounding in goodness and truth' " (Exodus 34:6).

Longsuffering is teamed up with mercy! As we read further, we will discover that it's not just a kind of mercy that merely covers something or is equal to its counterpart, but a mighty and abundant mercy.

"The LORD is longsuffering and abundant in mercy, forgiving iniquity and transgression" (Numbers 14:18a).

The King James Version says "of great mercy." The Hebrew word for **great** translates as *"abundant, exceedingly full, mighty, and to multiply."* It comes from the word which translates as *"to increase by many, to be more, by ten thousands."* This is the element that longsuffering is teamed up with— God's exceedingly complete, mighty, and ever-increasing mercy!

"But You, O Lord, are a God full of compassion, and gracious, longsuffering and abundant in mercy and truth" (Psalm 86:15).

The King James Version says "plenteous in mercy." God's mercy is often on full display when He chooses to be longsuffering. Admittedly, when going through life circumstances, we may not understand why God seems hesitantly slow to correct or judge those who have done us wrong. Could it be that God's mercy is being displayed to them (and to us) by giving a space for repentance?

Longsuffering is a product of God's love and mercy toward humanity. Longsuffering is the fruit that God chooses to challenge the enslaving roots of bitterness, hatred, impatience, and unforgiveness in our hearts. Longsuffering is the fruit that challenges our carnality. It also reveals the nature of God to us in a very personal way.

The verse stated that our God is *"abundant in mercy and truth."* One of the primary purposes for longsuffering is that it is a pathway to reveal the truth. That may be a personal revelation or a social revelation of truth. His purposes consistently demonstrate His compassion, grace, patience, mercy, and truth. But if we are only focused on the pain of our situation, we will miss the purpose of our situation. What does God desire to reveal to you and others? What life-changing testimony is God forging in you by giving you the grace to endure this situation instead of delivering you *from* the situation?

At the time of this publication, I have three beautiful children, ages 8, 6, and 2. I will be completely transparent: there are some days I don't like to "parent." There are days when my wife and I wish we could ship them off to their grandparents for their entire summer break. We must endure the continuous whining, crying, fighting, messes, temper tantrums, and dirty diapers—simply put, it drives us crazy some days! (Can I get a loud "AMEN" from all the parents of multiple children!?) But regardless of how much stress they put my wife and I through at times, our attitude is that unless we have permitted you to discipline our children, "don't **you** touch them!"

Nothing speaks more of our Heavenly Father's love, mercy, grace, and longsuffering than parenthood. As their parents, and as much as we must deal with their mistakes, messes, and mindsets—our love for them is so real and genuine. A simple "I love you, Daddy!" or a kiss on the  cheek for Mommy has the (annoying) power to wash away the past few moments of stress. As parents, we are willing (do we have any other option, really?) to "suffer long" with our children. Why? Because while we are currently stressing out because of their immaturity, we understand that growth and maturity *are* happening in parallel. The challenge is to endure and enjoy the advancing growth while dealing with the quarrels, arguments, and messy play areas often created anywhere in the house.

As I write this chapter in my office, I hear Kimberlyn, our oldest child, yell, "Mommy, Jerry (our middle child) just made a huge mess in the living room!" My wife, who is feeding lunch to the baby, Kaylee, responds, "Can you help him clean it up?" Without hesitation, Kim answers, "Yup!" She immediately went to the task of cleaning up. But, within a few moments, the two started arguing about which side of the mess was theirs to clean up. *Oh, brother!* This went on for a few moments.

I'm happy to report that, after some time and calming down, the mess *is* cleaned up. It happened without injury but not without argument. It wasn't a perfect clean-up situation, by far. But a few months ago, Kim may not have been so willing to help her brother clean up a mess that wasn't hers. While I'm transparently annoyed at the arguing, I am rejoicing that the mess *is* cleaned up, that Kim notified her mother of the situation, that she immediately helped her brother, and that her brother also helped clean the mess.

LONGSUFFERING DOES NOT MEAN THAT WE LET PEOPLE GET AWAY WITH STUFF! But, it does require us to be more patient, more controlled, and less impulsive in "bringing on the correction" when people make mistakes, argue with us, or make decisions we disapprove of.

Too often, we mistakenly view God's love and merciful longsuffering as God allowing people to "get away with" hurtful and sinful things. Believe me when I say God will enact His justice upon those guilty and refusing to repent.

"The Lord is longsuffering and abundant in mercy, forgiving iniquity and transgression; but He by no means clears the guilty ..." (Numbers 14:18b).

Knowing this truth will give us hopeful endurance through the injustices we face; however, I fear we have been too quick to seek God's vengeance on people for their injustices against us. In the height of our emotions, we often forget that He is a merciful God and may choose to show longsuffering to our offenders to give them a space to repent.

We must be mindful of a critical element when enduring longsuffering situations: **we must consider people's developmental stages,** including spiritual, mental, emotional, etc. This key will help liberate us from bitterness, anger, and revenge. I now understand the weight of this principle because I have a lifetime of parenting still before me.

One of the best moments of my life was when Kim took her first steps. As new parents, this was a big moment for us. She mastered the skill in just one day. Late in the morning, she took a step, and then she would fall. Then, a while later, she took two steps and fell. But she kept at it throughout that day and wouldn't give up.

When I returned home from work late that evening, she was excited to see Daddy because she is "Daddy's girl." My wife told me to take her favorite blanket to the opposite side of the room and see if Kim would walk over to me. Without any hesitation, Kim immediately stood up and walked from one end of the room to the other with the most beautiful, heartwarming smile as both my wife and I were proudly and loudly cheering her on. She grabbed the blanket from my hands, fell proudly at my feet, and let out a cheerful squeal. My wife and I were clapping, laughing, and crying all at the same time. It was a moment I will never forget, partially because I got it on video and because of the immense joy it gave us all.

Was I upset that she fell at my feet? Was I critical of her only being able to walk about 12 steps until she dropped to the floor? Absolutely not! I was caught up in the joy of the moment. She had learned and was mastering a significant life skill in just one day. I was enjoying the moment of her maturity while she still had to endure the momentum of falling to the floor.

If we are purposeful, *we can enjoy life while enduring life*. We can find joy in the midst of waiting for justice. We can also experience victory while waiting to be avenged. But this is a choice that must be made, sometimes on a daily basis. It's a matter of perspective and locking your focus onto heaven's purpose.

As parents, we understand that maturing is a long process (that includes many LONG days). What parent would put their kids up for adoption whenever they fight, argue, scream, have temper tantrums, splash water all over  the floor during bath time, push each other off the couch, fight over the remote, or cry over who gets tucked in bed first? I don't think you would, and certainly, our Heavenly Father would never do such a thing. He is a good, good Father. He chooses to be merciful, *abundantly merciful*, and forgiving as we mature.

Not only does He show mercy and forgiveness, but He rejoices over the small victories we achieve in our maturation. Even God is familiar with the pattern of longsuffering: enjoying the achievements while enduring the mistakes. Shouldn't we, as Christians (the "Christ-like" ones), do no less?

Years ago, I was ministering at a church, and we did an exercise to capture people's perspectives. This little exercise proved to be very effective and self-revealing. I called it "The Stone or the Starburst."

I invited everyone to come up front and asked them to remove one shoe, into which I then placed a tiny stone. I then instructed them to put their shoe back on. We then handed out a Starburst candy for each of them to chew on as they took three laps around the sanctuary.

The musicians played an uplifting song as they marched. You could see some struggling to walk, some laughed, others grunted, and some even complained. Some had twisted expressions on their faces—from the stone in their shoe or the Starburst's chewiness; we may never know. At the end of the third lap, I had them line up in the front.

I asked everyone to answer, "What were you more focused on, the stone in your shoe or the Starburst in your mouth?" Overwhelmingly, they confessed that they were focused much more on the small stone. They admitted that it was difficult to enjoy the sweetness of the Starburst candy in their mouth while dealing with the small, annoying pebble in their shoe.

The fundamental aim of this exercise was to assess their perspective regarding God's blessings (the Starburst) versus the annoyances we face in life (the small stone). How often do we lose sight of God's blessings, which we are to savor and enjoy because of the annoyances we must endure that inflict pain as we walk the paths of this life?

"Therefore we do not lose heart. Even though our outward man is perishing, yet the inward man is being renewed day by day. For our light affliction, which is but for a moment, is working for us a far more exceeding and eternal weight of glory" (2 Corinthians 4:16-17).

Much of this comes down to our **perspective** and how we, as individuals, choose to **persevere** in suffering. We  have a decision to make. Do we tend to whine, or do we truly worship? Do we seek a pity party, or do we sincerely praise Him? A preacher once said, "There are two depressing things about a pity party. Hardly anyone shows up, and no one brings gifts." Do we tend to focus on the little stone or the delicious Starburst?

God allows suffering or "light afflictions" because they are sent to our lives for blessing and benefit, not only for us but for others to experience the liberating power of truth. His grace, mercy, and truth are not only for our benefit but for the very ones who harmed and afflicted us. It is especially for those who are watching our lives unfold for the glory of God. What life-changing truth and revelation is God unlocking to others in your life or through your life?

Even if our afflictions last our entire lifetime, they remain "light afflictions" compared to an eternity in the raw and real presence of our Good, Good Father. Worst case scenario, what is one lifetime filled with unending affliction compared to a never-ending eternity with the Comforter, Healer, and Redeemer? Can we find hope today *for* tomorrow in the midst of our hurt?

I hear the old church song, *"Because He lives I can face tomorrow. Because He lives all fear is gone. Because I know He holds the future. And life is worth the living just because He lives"* (Bill and Gloria Gaither).

What tremendous life lessons we can learn concerning God's abundant mercy, grace, and truth revealed through exercising the fruit of longsuffering. We can be thankful that longsuffering is teamed up with abundant mercy. We can deal with the imperfect as we are in the process of being perfected. We can enjoy life while we endure and wait for God's truth and justice. What are you more focused on, His mercy or your mess? And even if the answers and God's avenging do not come to us as we expect them to, we can still rise above our current circumstances and fix our focus on eternity—one that is filled with victory, peace, joy, and freedom.

MAKE IT PERSONAL

1.) In reading the Scriptures in this chapter, what does the understanding that longsuffering is teamed up with mercy mean to you personally?

_____

_____

_____

_____

2.) Are you one who quickly seeks to avenge yourself or pray for God's vengeance on someone who has done you wrong? If so, has this chapter challenged you? Has your perspective begun to change? (See Luke 6:27-28, Romans 12:19-21, and Galatians 6:9)

_____

_____

_____

_____

3.) Imagine someone called on you to do "The Stone or the Starburst" exercise; which would you focus more upon? Given your answer, what does this exercise say to you about your perspective?

_____

_____

_____

_____

4.) Take a few moments to assess your current circumstance, pain, or affliction. Ask yourself how God can use this to reveal an aspect of truth and mercy to you, or to the one who hurt you, and to the very world you influence.

_____

_____

_____

_____

Stuart Holden, the author of "Prevailing Intercessory Prayer", was in Egypt and met a sergeant in a Highland regiment. "How were you brought to Christ?" he asked this bright Christian.

The sergeant responded: "There was a private in the same company as myself who had been converted in Malta, and I gave him a terrible time. I remember one night in particular when it was very rainy and he came in wet and weary from sentry duty. Yet, as usual, he still got down on his knees before going to bed.

My boots were covered in mud and I threw them both at him and hit him twice on the head. He kept kneeling and praying.

The next morning when I woke up I found my boots beautifully cleaned and polished at my bedside. This was his reply to me and it broke my heart. That day I was brought to repentance."

(Adapted from a sermon by Ken Pell, A Fruit-Full Marriage: Gentleness (Gentle Love), 9/4/2011)

Chapter 4

Overcoming Revenge

"It's difficult to think anything but pleasant thoughts while eating a homegrown tomato." ~ Lewis Grizzard

While checking his bags at the airport, a man became dissatisfied with the employee who handled the luggage. For  several minutes he belittled the young man and criticized his every move. Surprisingly, the curbside porter didn't seem troubled by this man's verbal abuse. After the angry man entered the airport, a woman approached the luggage handler and asked, "How do you put up with such injustice?"

The young man said, "It's easy. That guy's going to New York, but I'm sending his bags to Brazil." [11]

It is indeed a humorous story because it appeases our carnal urge for "justice." We have all faced harsh criticism to some measure at some point in our lives, so we can readily sympathize and relate to this young man's reaction. From our human perspective, the angry man "got what he deserved." Some of us would have done the same thing if we were honest.

But, to ask the classic question, "What would Jesus do?" How would Jesus have responded to this angry man who belittled and openly criticized him? An honest assessment of that question makes our carnality cringe at what Jesus would have done. If we are honest with ourselves, we would look over the experiences of life and say that we could use a little more help and grace to fulfill "… *love your enemies, bless those who curse you, do good to those who hate you, and pray for those who spitefully use you and persecute you*" (Matthew 5:44).

One of the reasons why many of us struggle to apply this verse, specifically the "love, bless, do good to, and pray for those," is we feel that somehow, by doing the *right thing* and taking the "high road" that we are letting the guilty party off the hook—that somehow, we are ignoring and condoning their distasteful and dishonorable behavior.

Immediately, the tendency is to seek "justice" and enact vengeance or punishment. They are waiting for "the day of reckoning" and the day that vengeance comes on their offender so that they can initiate  their payback. One of the key factors why people hold onto offenses for many years is because they feel that at some point, punishment *should be* passed, and "justice" should be served somewhere.

But seeking "payback" should not be a Christian's attitude; contrary to our human emotions, this is a sub-par way of living. *"Beloved, do not avenge yourselves, rather give place to wrath; for it is written, "Vengeance is Mine, I will repay," says the Lord"* (Romans 12:19). Admittedly, this is not easy for us to do. It takes self-control (temperance) to resist the urge to retaliate, strike back, and get even with our offender.

You can say, "It sounds like we are letting them off the hook." But the truth of the matter is, when we turn control of the situation over to God, we are, in essence, **taking them off of OUR hook … and placing them onto GOD'S hook.** Free up your hook by putting them on God's hook. It has been wisely said, "Forgiveness doesn't make them right; it just sets me free."

"… *bearing with one another, and forgiving one another, if anyone has a complaint against another; even as Christ forgave you, so you also must do*" (Colossians 3:13).

When people read verses like this, it can quickly bring apprehension or even create a stumbling block because the concept of forgiveness is an unacceptable option to them. "Why in the world would I ever have to forgive what they did to me? It was horrible, sinful, and even illegal?" Such a thing may be humanly impossible. Why would we even want to forgive the evil done to us? How could we ever forgive it? Why should we forgive it?

But we must understand that forgiveness is not about bypassing justice; it is about allowing God to execute His justice in a way and time that He sees fit and proper. God judges in perfect righteousness, and His judgments are carried out with perfection, precision, purity, and without partiality (see Psalm 50:6). Forgiveness is about letting people off our hook and putting them on the Judge's hook.

By doing this, we give Him a place to heal and help our hearts, and it brings us into a position of resolve and a release of anger toward the offender(s) and the circumstance.

Forgiveness is not about hiding the offense; it is about receiving healing from the offense. God does not expect us to be doormats or pincushions because, as Christians who follow and reflect Christ, He was neither of those things—yet He still chose to forgive. You may never forget the offense, but that doesn't mean it is impossible to forgive and be free from it. Forgiveness is not about feelings but an act of our will, lining up to His will and Word.

One Scripture that should motivate us not only to forgive, but to forgive quickly and very often is *"For if you forgive men their trespasses, your heavenly Father will also forgive you. But if you do not forgive men their trespasses, neither will your Father forgive your trespasses"* (Matthew 6:14-15).

No other Scriptures have I found (or needed) that motivates me to live in a place of constant and consistent repentance and forgiveness. These two verses should help deliver us from revenge-seeking. While my human nature longs for "justice and vengeance," I am reminded that my sin is ever before me (see Psalm 51). Furthermore, how I process the offenses of others toward me has a direct bearing on my relationship and standing with God.

Forgiveness is about releasing the offender from any obligation to pay you back and allowing God to repay you. *"Beloved, do not avenge yourselves, but rather give place to wrath; for it is written, "Vengeance is Mine, I will repay," says the Lord"*

(Romans 12:19). It has everything to do with releasing the offense and giving it to God, for Him to repay as He sees fit.

One of the most incredible things about forgiveness is that it does not require any action from your offender. You can forgive and extend mercy without any request from them to do so. You can be set free all by yourself—even if they have tried (or are still trying) to manipulate your emotions, actions, and thinking. Through forgiveness, it hinders that from happening. This one-way action puts everything into the hands of the Holy One!

The prophet Jeremiah prayed, *"O Lord, You know; Remember me and visit me, And take vengeance for me on my persecutors. In Your enduring patience* (KJV – "longsuffering"), *do not take me away. Know that for Your sake I have suffered rebuke"* (Jeremiah 15:15).

There is nothing like suffering for what God calls you to do. Sometimes, you will get accused; you will be slandered, hindered, harassed; you will be betrayed; you will be misrepresented, and maybe even downright hated. The urges and surges of emotions that come in those moments tempt you to strike back, get on social media, make a scene, and clear your name with Scripture and all such things. But we must realize that *God may be developing fruit* in the midst of

the storm. It is called longsuffering. Although it may not taste as sweet, it is a necessary fruit of the Spirit!

Malcolm Muggeridge once said, "Contrary to what might be expected, I look back on experiences that at the time seemed especially desolating and painful with particular satisfaction. Indeed, I can say with complete truthfulness that everything I have learned in my 75 years in this world, everything that has truly enhanced and enlightened my experience, has been through affliction and not through happiness."

Longsuffering helps me overcome pride and self-preservation. It tames the urge to fight back. It teaches me to rely on God's process and power. Longsuffering, above all, teaches me that the battle is the Lord's, not mine. Longsuffering teaches me how to release and let go, even when the sounds of the storm still rage, and at first, nothing may seem to change.

MAKE IT PERSONAL

1.) Would you be the person to send the rude man's bags to Brazil?

_____

_____

_____

_____

2.) Generally, are you a forgiving person? Reading Matthew 6:14-15, does this challenge you to make some necessary changes?

_____

_____

_____

_____

3.) Are you ready to let people "off your hook" and start putting them on "God's hook"? Do you trust God to avenge you and carry you through this situation once you give it to Him to do as He proposes?

_____

_____

_____

_____

4.) What does the statement "The battle is the Lord's, not mine!" mean to you personally?

_____

_____

_____

_____

5.) *You can be set free all by yourself!* How do you make yourself free? What does that look like?

_____

_____

_____

_____

"Unforgiveness is like drinking poison yourself
and waiting for the other person to die."
BRAINYQUOTE.COM

"Forgiveness is like letting go of a bell rope. If you have ever seen a country church with a bell in the steeple, you will remember that to get the bell ringing you have to tug awhile. Once it has begun to ring, you merely maintain the momentum. As long as you keep pulling, the bell keeps ringing.

Forgiveness is letting go of the rope. It is just that simple. But when you do so, the bell keeps ringing. Momentum is still at work. However, if you keep your hands off the rope, the bell will begin to slow and eventually stop."

- Corrie Ten Boom

Chapter 5

Mastering Endurance

"Two tomatoes went jogging. One trips and falls. The other tomato said, "Grab my Heinz and I'll help you up." Trippy tomato replies, "Hah, you go ahead. I'll ketchup." ~ Readbeach.com

Longsuffering challenges us to begin living and walking by faith. Very few things are more effective than longsuffering, which can stir us to confront and conquer our fears. It is longsuffering that influences us to mature and overcome wimpiness. Longsuffering teaches us endurance as we wait to attain the promises and blessings of God in our lives.

"For you have need of endurance, so that after you have done the will of God, you may receive the promise" (Hebrews 10:36).

The Greek word for "endurance" is *hypomonē*, which translates as *"cheerful (or hopeful) patience, constancy, a patient continuance in waiting."* It pictures someone not swerving from their purpose and loyal to their faith even in the greatest trials and sufferings.

Endurance is defined as *"the fact or power of enduring or bearing pain, hardships, etc. The ability or strength to continue or last, especially despite fatigue, stress, or other adverse conditions; stamina."* [12]

It has been widely stated that **FEAR** has two meanings: Forget Everything And Run, or Face Everything

And Rise! Fear has two definitions at opposite spectrums. Fear carries different value systems and conclusions. When confronted with fear, we must decide which meaning to apply to our lives and circumstances. As one Christian song declares, *"I'm no longer a slave to fear. I am a child of God."* (No Longer Slaves, by Bethel Music)

"Love is the key. Joy is love singing; peace is love resting; long-suffering is love enduring; kindness is love's touch; goodness is love's character; faithfulness is love's habit; gentleness is love's self-forgetfulness; self-control is love holding the reins." [13]

One of the biggest boxing matches of the twentieth century took place on November 25, 1980, at the Superdome in New Orleans, Louisiana. It was a rematch between Sugar  Ray Leonard and Roberto Duran. Duran had won the previous fight and was the favorite the second time around. He had a record of 72 wins and just one loss, and he had won his last 41 fights. The rematch was a close fight. Only a point or two separated the two fighters on the judges' scorecards. But then something unthinkable happened in the eighth round that no one expected. Roberto Duran turned to the referee and spoke two words: *"No Mas."* --- "No more!" He quit! He wasn't injured, and he wasn't cut. He was frustrated, and he just had enough!

Here is a fighter who was one of the best to ever step into the ring. He won a total of 103 fights, but when anyone mentions his name today, the first thing that comes to mind is "no mas." People remember the day he quit. [14]

If we are to be "Christ-like" people desiring to exemplify the nature of God, we cannot be quitters. I am so thankful that our God never fails and never quits. God doesn't intend for us to quit, throw in the towel, or disqualify ourselves in a defeatist or doubting mentality. This principle is demonstrated with the fruit of longsuffering being made available through the power of the Holy Spirit operating in our lives.

"And not only that, but we also glory in tribulations, knowing that tribulation produces perseverance; and perseverance, character; and character, hope" (Romans 5:3-4).

We need to have the same mindset as the cowboy Jedediah in the family movie *Night at the Museum*, when he shouted to the Roman General Octavius, "I AIN'T QUITTIN' YOU!" We should make up our minds and shout …

"Jesus— I ain't quittin' you!"

"My Family— I ain't quittin' you!"

"Truth— I ain't quittin' you!"

"Pastor— I ain't quittin' you!"

"Lost souls— I ain't quittin' you!"

We may be beaten up, bleeding, and frustrated in the fight— BUT WE "AIN'T QUITTIN' YOU!"

We cannot quit because God doesn't quit; it is not in His nature. His nature is to be activated and enhanced in our lives through the power of the Holy Spirit. What God starts, He intends to finish. He does not quit. He is going to finish what He began in us.

"Being confident of this very thing, that He who has begun a good work in you will complete it until the day of Jesus Christ" (Philippians 1:6).

"And the Lord, He is the One who goes before you. He will be with you, He will not leave you nor forsake you; do not fear nor be dismayed" (Deuteronomy 31:8).

As Christians who bear His name and possess His Spirit, we cannot allow ourselves to self-destruct by giving into doubt, depression, and despair. The enemy can manipulate us if we don't enhance our capacity to endure hardship. Sadly, if we never allow longsuffering to be added to our lives and we lack the spiritual stamina to remain faithful during seasons of pain, trouble, or suffering, it could ultimately become a life-or-death situation.

The tale is told about two frogs falling into a tub of cream. One looked at the tub's high sides, which were too difficult to crawl over, and said, "It is hopeless." So, he resigned himself to death, relaxed, and sank to the bottom. The other frog was much more determined and kept swimming as long as possible.  "Something might happen," he said. He kept kicking and churning, and finally, he found himself on a solid platform of butter and jumped to safety. [15]

"And let us not grow weary while doing good, for in due season we shall reap if we do not lose heart" (Galatians 6:9).

FEAR has two meanings. You can give up, surrender, and let your current circumstances overcome your mind, emotions, and spirit, or you can "keep on kicking" until your victory becomes a reality. We are fighting the good fight of faith. We have a choice to fight with faith or die with fear.

"O Timothy, you are God's man. Run from all these evil things, and work instead at what is right and good, learning to trust him and love others and to be patient and gentle. Fight on for God. Hold tightly to the eternal life that God has given you and that you have confessed with such a ringing confession before many witnesses" (1 Timothy 6:11-12 TLB).

Where do we go to receive comfort in times of trials, turmoils, and terrors? Where do we find something tangible to release hope in seemingly hopeless situations? There is no more excellent lifeline than the Word of God. You can literally hold onto it, stand on it, quote it, declare it, and defeat the enemy's lies with it!

"For whatever things were written before were written for our learning, that we through the patience (hypomonē) *and comfort of the Scriptures might have hope"* (Romans 15:4).

We can receive comfort and assurance that God can see us through by reading the real-life events of people in the pages of the Bible. They suffered pain, endured countless hardships, and experienced many losses. If we are honest with ourselves, we will see that these "heroes of faith" endured things that were much more severe than what we may be currently facing. It's on record that you are not alone in your suffering. We have 66 books of the Bible, filled with people who endured many trials and tribulations. However, if they stayed faithful, they experienced grace, provision, and, in many cases, deliverance. **God's purpose, plan, and power are shown through the broken cracks of their lives.**

Job suffered, perhaps unlike anyone else we read about in the entirety of Scripture. He lost everything—his children, health, wealth, and reputation. But he endured, kept his faith, and did not speak foolishly. Job suffered long. But the Scripture says, *"Now the Lord blessed the latter days of Job more than his beginning; for he had fourteen thousand sheep, six thousand camels, one thousand yoke of oxen, and one thousand female donkeys. He also had seven sons and three daughters. After this Job lived one hundred and forty years, and saw his children and grandchildren for four generations. So Job died, old and full of days"* (Job 12-13, 16-17).

David, one of the most famous people in the Bible, was no stranger to harsh times. He was destined to be king over Israel—called, chosen, and anointed by God. But he was  chased, hunted, threatened, and tormented by King Saul, who was consumed with jealousy. He always had to watch his back, constantly hide, was forced to live in caves, and had to survive on whatever food was available. David was anointed to be king but faced years of suffering and agony before it became a reality. How many times did David get tired, weary, and frustrated?

Scripture says that David stayed true to his profoundly intimate relationship with his God. *"I cry out to the Lord with my voice; with my voice to the Lord I make my supplication. I pour out my complaint before Him; I declare before Him my trouble"* (Psalm 142:1-2). David later went on to fulfill his destiny as one of the greatest and most respected kings in all of history.

Time and space do not allow us to talk about Joseph, Moses, Ruth, Jeremiah, and many other noteworthy people of the Old Testament. Since Adam and Eve's fall, we can readily see that suffering, pain, hardship, and loss are part of humanity's story of redemption. God does not waste our pain. He uses it for His glorification and purpose.

Our Savior was not exempt from suffering and hardship. Jesus is known as the "suffering Savior." In fact, hundreds of years before Christ came, the prophet Isaiah foresaw the Messiah's sufferings (see Isaiah 53:3-5). Christ had to suffer because of our sins. *So, if God Himself had to endure suffering in His life, how can we expect any less?* Whether you are a Christian or not, trials, tribulations, hardships, and suffering are part of humanity's story. If you are a human being, you are not exempt and will never be exempt. It is part of our story.

Jesus had to endure many things throughout His life—criticism from His hometown; schemes of entrapment from "religious teachers" the Pharisees and Sadducees; doubt, betrayal, and unbelief from His disciples. He endured a sadistic, horrendous beating just before His gruesome crucifixion. People rejected Him throughout His earthly life. Just before His  death, one thief hanging on the cross beside Him did not believe in Him. Thomas, one of Jesus' disciples, did not believe Jesus was resurrected until he personally encountered the resurrected Lord. Finally, James, the half-brother of Jesus, did not believe Jesus was the Messiah until *after* His resurrection (see John 7:5, 1 Corinthians 15:7, Acts 1:14).

Finally, let's talk about possibly the most spiritual and educated man in the New Testament, the Apostle Paul. He wrote at least 13 books of the New Testament and was definitely not exempt from enduring pain, hardship, and suffering. As a matter of fact, when you read his accounts of suffering, ask yourself how bad your current suffering is in comparison to what he faced throughout his life and ministry.

*"Are they serving Christ? I am serving him more. (I am crazy to talk like this.) I have worked much harder than they have. I have been in prison more often. I have been hurt more in beatings. I have been near death many times. **Five times** the Jews*

*have given me their punishment of 39 lashes with a whip. **Three*** ***different times** I was beaten with rods. **One time** I was almost killed with rocks. **Three times** I was in ships that were wrecked, and **one of those times** I spent the night and the next day in the sea. In my **constant traveling** I have been in danger from rivers, from thieves, from my own people, and from people who are not Jews. I have been in danger in cities, in places where no one lives, and on the sea. And I have been in danger from people who pretend to be believers but are not. I have done hard and tiring work, and **many times** I did not sleep. I have been hungry and thirsty. **Many times** I have been without food. I have been cold and without clothes. **And there are many other problems.** One of these is the care I have for all the churches. I worry about each group of believers every day. I feel weak every time another person is weak. I feel deeply upset every time another person is led into sin. If I must boast, I will boast about the things that show I am weak"* (2 Corinthians 11:23-30 ERV).

That was the most spiritual and educated guy in the room, who was saved by a persecuted Jesus while on his way to persecute Christians for their faith (see Acts 9). See, pain is part of everyone's story. Pain can still produce God's glorious purpose, plan, and power in our lives if we don't quit or throw in the towel and refuse to focus all our attention on the pain and problems. Pain has the power to instill in us a pursuit of Jesus, with more hunger and tenacity than we have ever experienced before.

Look at your life's root system. Has your life's pain, pressure, and problems uprooted you? Or have they deepened your dependency and relationship with Jesus?

The story is told that A. Parnell Bailey once visited an orange grove where an irrigation pump had broken down. The season was unusually dry, and some of the trees were beginning to die for lack of water. The man giving the tour then took Bailey to his own orchard, where irrigation was used sparingly. "These trees could go without rain for another two weeks," he said. "You see when they were

young, I frequently kept water from them. This hardship caused them to send their roots deeper into the soil in search of moisture. Now mine are the deepest-rooted trees in the area. While others are being scorched by the sun, these are finding moisture at a greater depth."

Pain can depress us or deepen us. Circumstances can make us bitter or bolster us into more incredible blessings. Suffering can make us surrender in defeat or make us surrender to Christ. Rest assured that our pain has a purpose, and God can use it for His glorious plan and purpose.

"And we know [with great confidence] that God [who is deeply concerned about us] causes all things to work together [as a plan] for good for those who love God, to those who are called according to His plan and purpose" (Romans 8:28 AMP).

MAKE IT PERSONAL

1.) **FEAR** has two meanings: Forget Everything And Run, or Face Everything And Rise! Which meaning have you typically chosen to apply to your life? Why?

_____

_____

_____

_____

2.) "If we are to be "Christ-like" people desiring to exemplify the nature of God, we cannot be quitters!" How does this statement challenge you?

_____

_____

_____

_____

3.) How can God redeem or use your current painful circumstances for His glory and ultimate purpose?

_____

_____

_____

_____

4.) Reading Paul's account of suffering in **2 Corinthians 11:23-30,** what does this say about the pain we face in our own lives?

_____

_____

_____

_____

5.) Look at your life's root system. Has your life's pain, pressure, and problems uprooted you? Or have they deepened your dependency and relationship with Jesus?

_____

_____

_____

_____

The only bird that dares to peck an eagle is the crow. The crow sits on the eagle's back and bites his neck. The eagle does not respond nor fight with the crow. It does not spend time or energy on the crow; instead, it just opens its wings and begins to rise higher in the heavens. The higher the flight, the harder it is for the crow to breathe, and eventually, the crow falls off due to a lack of oxygen.

Learn from the eagle, and don't fight the crows. Just keep ascending. They might be along for the ride, but they'll soon fall off. Do not allow yourself to succumb to the distractions— keep your focus on the things above and continue rising!

Author Unknown

63

Chapter 6

A Higher Purpose

"Canned tomatoes are like a summer saved; all the deep sun kissed flavors ready to be enjoyed." ~ Better Homes & Gardens

Do you struggle with impatience? Are you filled with anxiety over the unfinished, undone, and unfulfilled dreams of your life? Does the incomplete make you feel incompetent? Does the tarrying of God tempt you to trust in temporary solutions? If so, you are not alone!

As we wait for God's promises to be fulfilled, it would be wise to remember that **delay does not mean denial.** Be encouraged that "no" does not always mean "never" (see Acts 16:6, Acts 19:10). "Yes" does not mean "now" (see Genesis 17:15-19, 18:11-14). Though it may be the last thing we want to hear God say in times of immense pressure and pain… "wait" is a prevalent answer from God.

"Our soul waits for the Lord; He is our help and our shield" (Psalm 33:20).

Time is a creation of God (Genesis 1:14). For His purpose, God created heavenly lights for signs and to measure time with all its seasons (Ecclesiastes 3). Because God dwells in eternity (which surpasses and precedes time), He is not limited or confined to time, seasons, and deadlines. He can move and maneuver whatever He needs to do to bring your answer and His purpose into reality (see Joshua 10, 2 Kings 20, Matthew 24:29).

When we have no other option but to "wait" on the Lord to provide, answer, or fulfill His promise, we should remember that **delay does not mean denial**. If we are in a  "waiting period," that season of time must have a higher purpose than us merely attaining something. God is not hesitating, floundering, or struggling to come through for you. A higher purpose may be working within our awaited promise, and it is being dug out! Have you considered souls may be in the balance or a new spiritual pathway is being forged? All we are required to do is *prayerfully wait* while He works!

"The Lord is not slack concerning His promise, as some count slackness, but is longsuffering toward us, not willing that any should perish but that all should come to repentance" (2 Peter 3:9).

Peter reveals to us that God's delay has a higher purpose. When we catch a glimpse of His purpose while waiting for our anticipated promise, the pressure, the pain, and even suffering become a little more bearable. It all starts to take a backseat, and finally, we can ***begin to experience joy*** in what He is doing. God keeps His promises!

Another, more vivid translation of this verse says, *"He isn't really being slow about his promised return, even though it sometimes seems that way. But he is waiting [longsuffering], for the good reason that he is not willing that any should perish, and he is giving more time for sinners to repent"* (2 Peter 3:9 TLB).

This is a magnificent blessing for people who still struggle with inconsistency and hypocrisy, having bad days in which they do not act or react correctly, and are yet learning to lay aside every weight and sin. This verse reveals that God is *"forbearing, patient, bearing long with us, and he is not losing heart **toward us**."* Where would we be if God was hot-tempered, ready to judge us at the precise moment of every infraction? We would have no hope at all. His longsuffering toward us is the very thing that gives us space to repent, correct, and obtain mercy and grace.

Peter also reveals that God does not waste time. He is not slacking off. Before God fulfills His promise to us, He ensures everyone can "get in on it." He is making sure everything and everyone is in place. Longsuffering confronts impatience and our doubts concerning God's promises, timing, and overall plan for our lives. He works even when you don't see, feel, sense, or have evidence to hold on to.

Stan Telchin, a successful Jewish businessman, felt betrayed when his daughter, Judy, twenty-one, called home from college to say, "I believe Jesus is the Messiah."

To prove his daughter wrong, Telchin began an energetic quest for truth. So did Stan's wife, Ethel, and their other daughter, Ann. When the search created friction between Stan and Ethel, they agreed to pursue their studies independently.

Months later, Stan accepted an invitation to attend a National Convocation of Messianic Jews. He planned to "work the convention" just like any other business, meeting with anyone he thought could help him.

After a series of meetings, Stan lay awake in his dorm room, realizing he had arrived at a point of crisis. If the Bible was true—and he had concluded it was—then he really did believe in the God of Abraham, Isaac, and Jacob. He also admitted that he believed in the Bible as God's inspired Word. But he couldn't quite say, "Jesus is the Messiah."

He asked his roommate to pray for him. Art obliged, praying simply, "God, give Stan your peace and resolve his inner conflict."

The next morning at breakfast, a man at Stan's table asked him to pray before the meal. Startled by the request, Stan bowed his head and said: "Praised be Thou, O Lord our God, King of the universe. I thank you for the fellowship and the friendship at this table. I thank you for what we have learned at this meeting. I ask you now to bless this food, and I do so … in the name of **Jesus, the Messiah**."

For a moment, he sat there, amazed at what he had just prayed. The faces of others at the table were suddenly jubilant. "Stan," said one of them, "you're a believer!" One by one they got up from their seats and hugged Stan. Several cried with joy.

Stan began to weep too. He wasn't sure how his wife would take the news, but he called her, blurting out, "Ethel, honey, it's me. It's over. I've made my decision. Jesus is the

Messiah!"

There was a pause on the other line as Stan held his breath. Then his wife said softly, "Thank God! That makes it unanimous. We've all been waiting for you."

Stan's entire family—his wife and both daughters— had decided to trust Christ as the Messiah. Each had been praying and waiting patiently for the Holy Spirit of Christ to draw Stan into a relationship with himself. [16]

The joy of God's fulfilled purpose can and will make all the pain, pressure, and impatience "worth it" in the end.

I will never forget the message I heard from Pastor Michael Williams from Apopka, Florida, entitled *"The Left Hand of God."* He preached that throughout the Bible, we read about the "right hand of God." It symbolizes might, dominion, victory, strength, supernatural power, and ability. Nearly every book mentions, in one way or another, God's power, might, victory, strength, and supernatural ability– "the right hand of God." However, only one Scripture ever mentions the "left hand" of God.

Job was searching for answers to his suffering. He was looking for God, but he could not find Him. Yet, in Job's lamenting cry, he gave us a glimpse of something. Amid terror and torment, Job knew something about God that no other person within the pages of Scripture disclosed to us. Job declared, *"Behold, I go forward, but he is not there; and backward, but I cannot perceive him: On the left hand, where he doth work ..."* (Job 23:8-9a KJV).

Pastor Williams' sermon gave me a life-changing revelation, and it has challenged and shaped my entire perspective of God. It became evident that God's right hand  symbolizes His power, and His left hand symbolizes His procedure. God's right hand symbolizes His wonders, and His left hand symbolizes His working. God's right hand symbolizes His miracles, and His left hand symbolizes His managing. God's right hand symbolizes culmination, and His left hand symbolizes cultivation.

Therefore, if God is not demonstrating an instantaneous dynamic power in our lives, our miracle must be moving through a divine procedure. If God's wonders are not active in our lives, families, or churches—He must be working in our lives and the lives of our family and church members. We must allow Him to work and, if necessary, partner with Him. *What is God creating and cultivating?* He must be doing something fabulous and life-changing for you, which may affect many others.

This principle is revealed to us in the life of one of the most influential people in the New Testament (he wrote most of it), the Apostle Paul, previously known as Saul of Tarsus.

Saul of Tarsus was once a primary persecutor of the New Testament church. He was not an atheist who "didn't know better." He was a religious zealot. He was a highly educated Jew who believed in the One God but did not believe Jesus was the Messiah. He went around to the towns tormenting, arresting, and imprisoning Christians.

Saul carried authority because he permitted Stephen, the first Christian martyr, to be put to death. *"Now Saul was consenting to his death. At that time a great persecution arose against the Church which was at Jerusalem; and they were all scattered throughout the regions of Judea and Samaria, except the apostles. And devout men carried Stephen to his burial, and made great lamentation over him. As for Saul, he made havoc of the Church, entering every house, and dragging off men and women, committing them to prison"* (Acts 8:1-3).

The next chapter, Acts 9, describes his conversion: on his way to Damascus to arrest Christians, *"suddenly a light shone around him from heaven. Then he fell to the ground, and heard a voice saying to him, "Saul, Saul, why are you persecuting Me?" And he said, "Who are You, Lord?"* (Acts 9:3-5a).

This highly educated religious zealot, a One God Jew well versed in the Scripture, was shocked, surprised, and stunned. This man, passionate about God, momentarily lost his master's degree and became like a little child when he asked, *"Who are You, Lord?"* Suddenly, his education, tradition, and religious formats were interrupted.

"Who are You, Lord?" The word "Lord" is the Greek word *kyrios*, which translates *"Lord or Master."* It appears 748 times in the New Testament. It is someone who carries *supreme authority, control, or the power to decide*. It is also used as *the title given to God, the Messiah*.

Quite literally, Saul asked, *"Who are You, Messiah?"* A voice came from the light, *"I am Jesus, whom you are persecuting..."* (Acts 9:5). This was Saul's pivoting, life-changing moment. Everything he had learned, practiced, proclaimed, and even persecuted and imprisoned people over was now personalized in a persecuted Savior.

This Scripture reveals that persecuted Christians are not alone. The perpetrators are also persecuting God Himself. Jesus said, *"Saul, Saul, why are you persecuting **Me?**"* He did not say, *"Why are you persecuting my children (or my church)?"* He is showing us that we, the church, are His body (*see* Romans 12:4-5; 1 Corinthians 12:12, 27; Colossians 1:18). God takes our persecution, pain, and suffering personally, especially when we are enduring it in defense of holiness and truth.

As we continue reading the Book of Acts, we read that Paul repented, prayed fervently, obeyed the gospel, was converted, and became one of the most prolific New Testament gospel preachers and missionaries, first to the Jews and then more broadly to the Gentiles (non-Jewish people). As stated in our last chapter, he single-handedly wrote at least 13 books of the New Testament. The long-term effects of Paul's life, conversion, and ministry still impact people thousands of years later.

Let us think about this for a moment: **What was more beneficial to the Church and the Kingdom of God in the long term?** God removing, punishing, and striking down the vicious persecutor of His body, or saving and converting this same man and using His life's story, education, experience, and testimony to be the catalyst to launch an international, multicultural ministry?

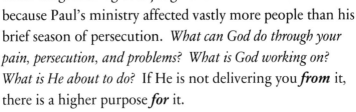

Paul was thankful God chose longsuffering over judgment because Paul's ministry affected vastly more people than his brief season of persecution. *What can God do through your pain, persecution, and problems? What is God working on? What is He about to do?* If He is not delivering you *from* it, there is a higher purpose *for* it.

Are you willing to endure a season of suffering (like the early Christians) to see someone else experience salvation and expand the Kingdom? The hard truth is that my pain is **secondary** to the purpose of God. God values His *eternal* purpose over my *temporary* problems. His goal is that none should perish, but all come to repentance.

Hear Paul's stirring testimony: *"For I would have you know, brothers and sisters, that the gospel which was preached by me is not of human invention. For I neither received it from man, nor was I taught it, but I received it through a revelation of Jesus Christ.*

For you have heard of my former way of life in Judaism, how I used to persecute the Church of God beyond measure and tried to destroy it; and I was advancing in Judaism beyond many of my contemporaries among my countrymen, being more extremely zealous for my ancestral traditions. But when He who had set me apart even from my mother's womb and called me through His grace was pleased to reveal His Son in me so that I might preach Him among the Gentiles, I did not immediately consult with flesh and blood, nor did I go up to Jerusalem to those who were apostles before me; but I went away to Arabia, and returned once more to Damascus.

Then three years later I went up to Jerusalem to become acquainted with Cephas, and stayed with him for fifteen days. But I did not see another one of the apostles except James, the Lord's brother. (Now in what I am writing to you, I assure you before God that I am not lying.) Then I went into the regions of Syria and Cilicia. I was still unknown by sight to the churches of Judea which are in Christ; but they only kept hearing, **"The man who once persecuted us is now preaching the faith which he once tried to destroy."** <u>**And they were glorifying God because of me**</u>*"* (Galatians 1:11-24 NASB).

Do not lose heart in the gloom because God's glory will break forth. Your pain and persecution can become the very platform that reveals God's glory to those your life impacts. Your suffering has saving and sanctifying power. *HE IS WORKING. LET HIM WORK!*

MAKE IT PERSONAL

1.) Have you considered God's patience concerning your life? What area of your life has God shown you the most patience? What does God showing you longsuffering entail?

_____

_____

_____

_____

2.) Do you see any similarities between Stan's and Apostle Paul's conversion experiences? If so, what are they? If not, where are the differences?

_____

_____

_____

_____

3.) Have you ever considered that Paul's preaching and ministry outweighed his persecution of the church? What does this mean to you personally?

_____

_____

_____

_____

4.) What can God do through your pain, persecution, and problem? What is God working on? What is He about to do?

_____

_____

_____

_____

5.) How can we experience *joy* through longsuffering?

_____

_____

_____

_____

*If He is not delivering you **from** it, there is a higher purpose **for** it!*

Years after the death of President Calvin Coolidge, this story came to light. In the early days of his presidency, Coolidge awoke one morning in his hotel room to find a burglar going through his pockets. Coolidge spoke up, asking the burglar not to take his watch chain because it contained an engraved charm he wanted to keep.

Coolidge then engaged the thief in quiet conversation and discovered he was a college student who had no money to pay his hotel bill or buy a ticket back to campus. Coolidge counted $32 out of his wallet-which he had also persuaded the dazed young man to give back! He declared it to be a loan, and advised the young man to leave the way he had come so as to avoid the Secret Service!

(Yes, the loan was paid back.)

Today in the Word, October 8, 1992

Chapter 7

To Reign Your Power

"I'm a tomato freak, but sometimes you have to get it in ketchup form for people to be open to tomatoes." ~ Tori Adams

Could you imagine the Bible without the Apostle Paul's writings? Could you imagine what Titus and Timothy and centuries of Christians would do without the mentorship of the Apostle Paul? As discussed in the previous chapter, he was, at one time, the most prominent and vicious persecutor of the New Testament church. After his encounter with Jesus on the road to Damascus (Acts 9), he obeyed the gospel, was converted, and became one of the most prolific preachers and missionaries this world has ever known.

Paul wrote a letter to Timothy, his son in the gospel and pastor of the church in Ephesus. Paul gave Timothy (and us) insight into God's higher purpose for sparing his life on the Damascus road. For generations to come, God intended to use Paul's life as a redemptive reminder.

"This is a faithful saying and worthy of all acceptance, that Christ Jesus came into the world to save sinners, of whom I am chief. However, for this reason I obtained mercy, that in me first Jesus Christ might show all longsuffering, as a pattern to those who are going to believe on Him for everlasting life. Now to the King eternal, immortal, invisible, to God who alone is wise, be honor and glory forever and ever. Amen" (I Timothy 1:15-17).

The word "longsuffering" here is the Greek word *makrothymia*, which translates as *"determination, longanimity, resilience, patience, and fortitude."* Upon further study, it depicts someone who *has the power to avenge but refrains from doing so.*

I can imagine the Apostle Paul saying, "Every day I wake up, I realize I deserved judgment, but instead, God showed longsuffering and mercy towards me." Paul knew that if it wasn't for God's longsuffering and mercy, his life could have been destroyed as he lay on the Damascus road, helpless, dazed, blinded, and perplexed.

Where would we be today without God's longsuffering and mercy toward us?

Does your offender deserve God's longsuffering and mercy? Does the person who has hurt, harassed, and harnessed your dreams deserve the same chance of attaining mercy? Saul was callous, cruel, and brutal to these "Christians" who were the first to receive God's mercy, grace, and salvation message. *But does Saul get a chance at mercy?* If we have a burden for souls to be saved, that should include our enemies.

WHO IS YOUR SAUL?

It would not amaze me if some first-century Christians in Jerusalem earnestly prayed for God to remove Saul due to the violence, viciousness, and devastation he caused the early church, comprised of many families. Homes where people gathered to worship were likely destroyed. People were scattered across the region. They had no other option but to pack up and move because of the intensity of persecution (Acts 8:1).

God could have avenged these Christians for losing their homes and for their family members who were tortured, imprisoned, or killed because of their faith. But instead of **removing** Saul, Jesus **revealed** Himself to Saul. God showed longsuffering and mercy to Saul. *God had the power to avenge, but He refrained from doing so.*

Jesus stopped Saul in his tracks. Through His longsuffering, God did not allow Saul to progress any

further. Through His merciful longsuffering, God was putting an end to the suffering and carnage caused by this particular persecutor. God's merciful act stopped Saul's momentum. Instead of avenging, God interrupted Saul's plans, invaded his belief system, and commissioned him beyond his current worldview.

*"This is a faithful saying and worthy of all acceptance, that Christ Jesus came into the world to save sinners, of whom I am chief. However, for this reason I obtained mercy, that in me first Jesus Christ might show all **longsuffering** [having the power to avenge, but refrains from doing so], as a pattern to those who are going to believe on Him for everlasting life"* (I Timothy 1:15-16).

The word "pattern" is the Greek word *hypotyposis*, which translates as *"a figure, a sketch, an example, an outline, a typification after."* It is used only two times in the Bible.

Thayer's Greek Lexicon defines it as *"the pattern placed before one to be held fast and copied or modeled after."* In essence, Paul is saying, "The same longsuffering and mercy shown at my conversion will not be lacking to anyone else who believes in the future." Paul's conversion experience shows us just how far God will go to save a soul, even the most vicious, cruel, and mistaken.

It may look like evil people get away with things, but God sees and knows all. He can interrupt them and put an end to their power and influence. If they don't repent and expose their hearts and lives to Jesus, they will be exposed one day.  But are we merely praying for revenge, or are we praying for their redemption?

*"Now as Jannes and Jambres resisted Moses, so do these also resist the truth: men of corrupt minds, disapproved concerning the faith; but they will progress no further, for their folly will be manifest to all, as theirs also was. **But you** have carefully followed my doctrine, manner of life, purpose, faith, longsuffering, love, perseverance, persecutions, afflictions, which happened to me at Antioch, at Iconium, at Lystra—what persecutions I endured. **And out of them all the Lord delivered***

me. Yes, and all who desire to live godly in Christ Jesus will suffer persecution" (2 Timothy 3:8-12).

Evil never wins. At some point, they will "progress no further." But until God delivers us out of them, we must endure. We may have to endure a season of suffering and experience a period of pain and hardships, but He will see us through.

A sprawling, shade-bearing, eighty-year-old American elm in Oklahoma City, Oklahoma, is a huge tourist

Photo Credit: Wikipedia

attraction. People pose for pictures beneath her. Arborists carefully protect her. She adorns posters and letterhead. The city treasures the tree, not because of her appearance but her endurance.

She made it through the Oklahoma City bombing. Timothy McVeigh parked his death-laden truck only yards from her. His malice killed 168 people, wounded 850, destroyed the Alfred P. Murrah Federal Building, and buried the tree in rubble. No one expected it to survive. No one gave any thought to the dusty, branch-stripped tree.

But then she began to bud. Sprouts pressed through damaged bark; green leaves pushed away gray soot. Life rose from an acre of death. People noticed. The tree modeled the resilience the victims desired. So they named her "The Survivor Tree." [17]

Trauma comes. Relationships break down and sever. People leave by death or by walking out the door. People die, from babies to elders. Businesses shut down. Pink slips show up. Offenses come. People get angry, then say and do things they later regret. Pain is part of our story. These tragedies shake and shatter our hearts, strip us of trust, and lay us bare and raw in our emotions; they can be so severe that they physically make us scatter.

Acts 11:19 tells us that people's lives were turned upside down due to Saul's persecution, that they had to uproot themselves: *"Now those who were scattered after the persecution that arose over Stephen traveled as far as Phoenicia, Cyprus, and Antioch, preaching the word to no one but the Jews only."* The Bible also tells us that *"the disciples were first called Christians in Antioch"* (Acts 11:25).

When you read Acts 11, it reveals something life-changing. Why was this particular body of believers labeled the *"first called Christians"*? What distinguished this gathering of people, or local church, from the rest of the churches also started because of the severe persecution?

Was it a revival? According to verses 20-21, the church in Antioch was having a revival amongst the Hellenists, or Greek-speaking Jews. A significant number of them believed and turned to Jesus. These believers in Antioch, who came from Jerusalem, were now going beyond themselves and their comforts and impacting their community. Was this why they were *"first called Christians"*?

Maybe, but the story continues. *"Then Barnabas departed for Tarsus to seek Saul. And when he had found him, he brought him to Antioch…"* (verses 25-26a).

"Wait … hold up! Barnabas, you mean you went *looking for* the person who ripped our families, homes, and hearts apart—*and brought him back here with you??*"

"Maybe I misunderstood you. You're telling me that you brought back the man who beat me, tortured me, and caused permanent damage to my legs so I can never walk again correctly? *Why, Barnabas? Why is he here??*"

"Barnabas, why would you bring him to us? I lost my husband, my son, and my daughter-in-law. I lost my beautiful home in Jerusalem, which was passed down from my parents. They nearly destroyed my entire family, except for my four grandchildren, who I am now raising. *Why would you do this??*"

"Aba and Imma (i.e., father and mother) were put in prison and killed for their faith in Jesus. I'm the eldest son, I'm only 14, and I have to work so much harder to care for my three younger siblings ever since our parents were taken. We barely escaped! We live with Nana now, but she is old and sickly, too. *Barnabas, I'm so scared he is here!*"

These are just a few examples of what may have run into the minds and hearts of the believers in Antioch when a converted, saved, and softer Saul of Tarsus entered their presence for the first time. Imagine the conflict, the raw emotion, and the flashbacks of terror, torture, and torment they endured—**BECAUSE OF HIM!**

"We are having a revival in our community. We are growing in faith and connections with new believers. Life has been hard, but it is finally starting to look a little better. We are still adjusting to our new homes, gathering places, and relationships—*WHY WOULD YOU BRING HIM HERE!?!*"

Anger. Anguish. Anxiety. Bitterness. Fear. Flashbacks. Phantom pains. Post Traumatic Stress. Hearing the screams of their loved ones being tortured viciously, carried away, and killed. The memories of many graveside ceremonies sent a chill down into their souls. No doubt some left the room to collect themselves; others may have left and didn't return.

Before Saul enters the room, Barnabas assures people that Saul has changed. He tells them briefly of his experience with Jesus on the road to Damascus—how Saul preached Jesus and the Jews wanted to kill him but escaped. He tells them that the disciples in Jerusalem were initially afraid to meet him but heard him preach, and now they welcome him.

Barnabas is about to say more… when a humble, anxious, converted Saul of Tarsus slowly enters the room with his head held low. The room is so quiet. All you can hear is the shifting of feet and the distant bustle of the city street. Saul takes his place next to Barnabas, with tears swelling in his eyes. He slowly lifts his head to look at the crowd, unsure what to expect.

Faces full of terror and tears sweep the room. The atmosphere is suddenly tangible and tense. Lips quiver, soft groans and sobs pierce through the silence. They are standing face to face with the person who wrecked their homes, families, and lives. Saul stood there weeping, trying to control himself. Through all his guilt, turmoil, shame, and embarrassment, Saul says, "Brothers and sisters, I greet you in the name of Jesus, the Messiah."

With that, the room erupts in relief and praise. In a few short moments, the presence of God fills the room. The Holy Spirit starts to minister peace and strength to everyone where they stand. Tears of anguish soon turn into tears of anticipation. Tears of loss are turned into love. Tears of grief turn into tears of gladness.

Barnabas lifts his voice and says, *"A new commandment I give to you, that you love one another; as I have loved you, that you also love one another. By this all will know that you are My disciples, if you have love for one another"* (John 13:34-35). The crowd rejoices and praises God with lifted hands.

After a few moments, a weeping old man slowly starts toward Saul. He is limping, leaning on his crutch, struggling, and wincing in pain. It was the man who was severely beaten and tortured. He had a notion to leave when Saul entered the room, but something within his spirit compelled him to stay. He stretches his hand out to Saul with tears in his eyes and, with love in his heart, compassionately says, "Welcome to Antioch, our brother Saul."

Recognizing the man, Saul quickly embraces him. Through his tears, Saul says, "Blessings be to you, my brother. Please, please forgive me." Surprised at the quick embrace, the old man starts to laugh, wrapping his arm around Saul, and says, "I already have forgiven you." The two men stand there weeping, embracing, and begin to laugh together.

Joy fills the room when Jesus fills the room! Before that day was over, Saul greeted every believer. There was peace. There was forgiveness. There was closure. Here is where *"Christians"* were born.

"So it was that for a whole year they [Barnabas and Saul] assembled with the church and taught a great many people. And the disciples were first called Christians in Antioch" (Acts 11:26b).

Their act of forgiveness was not a surface, half-hearted, save-face-in-church kind of forgiveness. It was the genuine article. It was the real deal. *Imagine the scene:* people gathering continuously (for a whole year) to be taught by a man once their greatest harasser, terrorizer, and persecutor.

That is "something you don't see every day." That is a glorious picture of Jesus at work. Only God can do such things. What does being a "Christian" mean? To *love and obey* God above all, and to *go beyond and love beyond* yourself. You forgive (from the depths of your heart) those who have hated you, hurt you, harassed you, and caused you to suffer long. Because through it all, **GOD STILL DOES AMAZING WORKS!**

MAKE IT PERSONAL

◆•————————•————————•◆

1.) **Who is your "Saul"?** Ask yourself: *"Do they deserve a chance at God's longsuffering and mercy? Do they deserve a chance at a personal encounter with Jesus?"*

_____

_____

_____

_____

2.) God showed longsuffering and mercy to Saul, meaning *"to have the power to avenge but refrains from doing so."* God reigned in his power; how can we reign in our power to avenge?

_____

_____

_____

_____

3.) Paul's conversion experience shows how far God will go to save a soul, even the most vicious, cruel, and mistaken. What does this mean to you personally and about your offenders?

_____

_____

4.) Why were the believers who lived in Antioch *"first called Christians"*?

_____

_____

_____

_____

5.) Paul Boose once said, *"Forgiveness does not change the past, but it does enlarge the future."* What does this statement create in your mind, emotions, and faith?

_____

_____

_____

_____

"Forgive others as quickly
as you expect God to forgive you."
GRACIOUSQUOTES.COM

Jenny Thompson has won ten Olympic medals in swimming, eight of which are gold. However, she didn't win any of the golds in individual events; she won them in team events with three other swimmers.

As a result, some people have questioned whether Jenny's swimming accomplishments ought to rank her with the "great" Olympic champions. She asks that herself. "It's got to be very different to experience an individual gold versus a team gold," she says.

I find Jenny's accomplishments in the ego-driven United States culture refreshing. With ballplayers moving from team to team, demonstrating little team loyalty, Jenny is a marvelous example of someone whose genuine success came in the context of team play.

This is how the Church should work. Our true "stardom" occurs when we participate as part of a winning team. On God's team, there is no room for superstars or mega-celebrities who do it on their own.

— Jon Mutchler,
"Jenny Thompson's Gold-Medal Teamwork," PreachingToday.com

Chapter 8

Overture Of Unity

"A person who thinks tomatoes grow on trees has in fact never been to a garden once." ~ Quotes Gram

There are two Hebrew words for "longsuffering" in the Old Testament. There are two Greek words for "longsuffering" in the New Testament. Both Greek words originate from the same word that shows a ***strong and zealous passion that is under control.***

"I, therefore, the prisoner of the Lord, beseech you to walk worthy of the calling with which you were called, with all lowliness and gentleness, <u>with longsuffering, bearing with one another in love, endeavoring to keep the unity of the Spirit</u> in the bond of peace" (Ephesians 4:1-3).

Other Bible translations of this text say, "make every effort," "being diligent," "striving to," "take every care," and "do your best … to keep UNITY!"

That sixteen-ounce jar of honey in your pantry exists only because *tens of thousands of bees* flew some 112,000 miles in a relentless pursuit of nectar gathered from *4.5 million flowers*. Every one of those foraging bees was female. By the time each died—living all of 6 weeks during honey-making season—she had flown about 500 miles in 20 days.

As these bees were flying themselves to death, production inside the hive continued with stupendous efficiency, as follows: A bee brings nectar to the hive, carried tidily in her "honey stomach." The bee is greeted by a younger, homebody receiver bee, who relieves her of her load. A receiver bee

 deposits nectar into a cell, reducing its water content and raising its sugar level by fanning it with her wings and regurgitating it up to 200 times, killing microbes along the way. More bees surround this cell and others and fan them with their wings 25,000 times or so, turning nectar into honey. When the honey is ripe, wax specialists arrive to cap off the cells. That is how every single ounce of every single honey pot, bottle, or jar in the world—hundreds of thousands of them—is brought into being.

"Every gulp of raw honey is a distinct, unique, unadulterated medley of plant flavor; a sweet, condensed garden in your mouth," writes Holley Bishop. [18]

God told Moses, *"So I have come down to rescue them from the power of the Egyptians and lead them out of Egypt into their own fertile and spacious land. It is a land flowing with milk and honey—the land where the Canaanites, Hittites, Amorites, Perizzites, Hivites, and Jebusites now live"* (Exodus 3:8).

What can we learn from this one verse? Two things are apparent. First, God never told Moses, "When I save and deliver you from Pharaoh (a type of Satan, sin, and the world system), your problems will be over." God was saving and delivering them from bondage in one location (Egypt) to partner with them to conquer and rule in another (the Promised Land). The children of Israel would not fight the Canaanites, Hittites (and all the other "ites") by natural means but with supernatural power working with them. Essentially, they would "rule and reign" with God in the land, be victorious, and live in abundant blessings if they stayed faithful and obedient to God's instructions.

Conflict doesn't end when we are saved and delivered; often, it intensifies. But through applying the gospel (see 1 Corinthians 15:1-4, Acts 2:36-39), we now are given spiritual power and authority to begin a journey of supernatural life and dominion. The Holy Spirit in our lives causes us to be *"more than conquerors"* (Romans 8:37). A life consumed and consecrated with the Holy Spirit has the potential to become more victorious than ever before. Conflict doesn't stop after salvation, but when we partner with Jesus and let Him fight our battles, the future looks bright, and the possibilities are endless.

Secondly, God was sending them to conquer a *"land flowing with milk and honey."* Milk must be extracted from the animal by something or someone else. Honey is produced by the efforts of many bees working together. This tells us that if we are going to attain our promised destiny, we must go through a process where things must be removed from us (by something or someone else). It also tells us that we need to get in partnership with things that are much bigger than we are.

If we are honest, we have been tempted to withdraw from people when precious things are removed, stripped, or extracted from us. We quickly and quietly retreat. We focus on "self-preservation." There is nothing wrong with biblically processing hurt. However, we often tend to focus on our wounds and offenses far too long; when we do, we lose focus on God's bigger picture and the commission to which we are called.

Offenses constitute a significant affront to unity. They must be handled quickly and biblically (that's another book for another time). Forgiveness is critical to maintaining agreement and peace in any relationship—spouses, children, family members, friendships, church members, co-workers, business partners, etc.

A traveler was making his way with a guide through the jungles of Burma. They came to a shallow, wide river and waded through it to the other side. When the traveler came out of the river, numerous leeches were on his torso and legs. His first instinct was to grab them and pull them off.

This guide stopped him, warning that doing so would leave tiny pieces of the leeches under the skin. Eventually, infection would set in. The best way to rid the body of the leeches, the guide advised, was to bathe in a warm balsam bath for several minutes. This would calm the leeches, and soon they would release their hold on the man's body.

Likewise, when I've been hurt by another person, I cannot simply yank the injury from myself and expect that all bitterness, malice, and emotion will be gone. Resentment still hides under the surface. The only way to become truly free of the offense and to forgive others is to bathe in the soothing bath of God's forgiveness. [19]

With Jesus in our focus, resentment, bitterness, envy, and anger should be subdued. It is not a righteous witness for our lives to be riddled with resentment, swallowed with scowls, eaten with evil contention, or absorbed in acid. When we can finally grasp the extent of God's love revealed in the life of Jesus Christ, forgiveness toward others should begin to flow from the depths of our hearts.

If you are a Christian, you are responsible for protecting the unity of your relationships, home, church,  workplace, and community to the best of your ability. Unity is so essential that the New Testament gives more attention to it than Heaven or Hell. Unity is the very soul of fellowship. Destroy unity; it will be as if you rip the heart out of Christ's body. It is the very essence of how God intends us to experience life together as His people.

"That you may walk worthy of the Lord, fully pleasing Him, being fruitful in every good work and increasing in the knowledge of God; strengthened with all might, according to His glorious power, for all patience and longsuffering with joy; giving

thanks to the Father who has qualified us to be partakers of the inheritance of the saints in the light" (Colossians 1:10-12).

Some believe unity is attained when everyone is "getting along" to the point of no disagreements, differences of opinion, or variations of administrations. While this belief is wonderful to imagine, it will most likely never be obtained. Even Jesus' disciples came from various occupations and backgrounds, ranging from fisherman to tax collector. Jesus even called a Zealot to follow Him; Simon was deeply involved in politics and government affairs of the day.

I can only imagine the untold stories and conversations between the disciples as they followed Jesus together. How did each view the world before following the Light of the world? How did they envision the Messiah and His triumphs? What family stories, suspicions, and secrets did each of them carry? Jesus called these men from various places, occupations, and world views to follow Him in agreement to discover the Kingdom of God.

It would be safe to conclude that if unity is about everyone being precisely alike in their points of view, perspectives, and perceptions, Jesus would not have handpicked most of these men to follow Him. He would have more likely picked people from an isolated family, vocation, or social status. But this is not what Jesus did. Therefore, unity goes beyond perspective. Unity has everything to do with **operating in agreement for a purpose**, not the unanimity of a specific practice or perspective.

The objective of playing on a baseball team is to work together to win games. But not everyone is a pitcher, a baseman, or an outfielder. Everyone has different positions on the team, working for the common purpose of winning the game. Each player brings unique skills, speed, and insight to the team. The real enjoyment is learning  to harness all this power, potential, and perspective into a winning baseball team. The team will not function if everyone has a catcher's mindset. There is much more to the game than that. Again, unity has everything to do with *operating in agreement for a purpose*, not the unanimity of a specific practice or perspective.

In his sermon, *Protecting Your Church*, Pastor Raymond Woodward shared some practical yet insightful principles on unity. (The comments in parentheses below are mine.)

- **Be Practical While Reaching Your Potential.** (Nothing destroys unity faster than unrealistic, impractical, and unobtainable expectations.)

- **Divorcing Your Church Over Little Issues Shows Immaturity.** (Everyone has issues, ranging from very little to very large. If everyone has issues, we can expect that every home, church, business, project, and organization will have some issues. Issues are part of life. Though they may be inconvenient, we should not disconnect ourselves over fixable issues.)

- **Rivalry Destroys Unity.** (It is unfortunate to see strife, envy, jealousy, and bitterness destroy good people who are called to put away the works of the flesh and begin to walk in the Spirit (Galatians 5:19-21).)

- **Our Focus Should Be on Common Ground, Not Our Differences.** (Common ground should include the gospel of Jesus Christ, worshipping and serving Jesus, evangelizing unsaved souls, blessing others, and enriching our communities by meeting physical and spiritual needs.)

- **We Should Value and Enjoy Our Differences.** (Life would be very unusual, chaotic, dull, and boring if everyone were just like me and just like you. Variety truly is the spice of life. Joy and intrigue come through learning and challenge.)

- **God Wants Unity, Not Uniformity.** (This point can not be overstated. God desires agreement and togetherness. Just as the physical body has many distinct members, they all work together. Each has its location, function, size, and purpose, but all work collectively for an ultimate purpose.)

- **Never Stoop to Snoop.** (Stay out if you are not part of the problem or the solution, no matter how intriguing the situations or conversations happening around you. Do not borrow trouble.)

- **Remember That People Who Gossip TO You Will**

Gossip ABOUT You. (The old saying is "no honor among thieves." The same is true about gossipers and complainers. No one who fellowships with people having uncontrolled emotions and loose lips is safe.)

- **Some People Grow Old, but They Never Grow Up.** (I'm going to leave that one... right here.)

- **Hell Can't Prevail Against a Unified Church.** (The people building the Tower of Babel made God admit, *"The people are united, and they all speak the same language. After this, nothing they set out to do will be impossible for them"* (Genesis 11:6 NLT). If ungodly people become unstoppable when they unify and focus on a single purpose, what can Spirit-filled people do once *they* become unified, working together for God's purpose?)

Having the fruit of longsuffering operating in our lives is how unity is attained and can be adequately maintained. Understanding that life and people are imperfect, offenses will come, and pain is part of our story will help keep our eyes on God's eternal purpose rather than on our temporary pain.

"Therefore, as the elect of God, holy and beloved, put on tender mercies, kindness, humility, meekness, longsuffering; bearing with one another, and forgiving one another, if anyone has a complaint against another; even as Christ forgave you, so you also must do" (Colossians 3:12-13).

In John 17, in His final moments before He was arrested and taken to Calvary, Jesus prayed passionately (in His last recorded prayer before His crucifixion) for our UNITY. Our unity was paramount in His mind during His most agonizing hours.

Nothing on earth is more valuable to God than His church, which comprises people and families. *IT'S THE ONLY THING IN THE ENTIRE WORLD HE HAD TO PAY FOR!* He paid the highest price for it, His blood, and He wants it protected. If you are part of His family, it is your responsibility to guard and protect it.

If God values us this much, we should think twice before devaluing each other. Let us pray diligently for a sincere love for people that goes deeper than our current suffering. May we learn to love beyond ourselves. May you bear the fruit of longsuffering, and I pray it be the pathway to the greatest joys your life will ever experience. *DON'T QUIT … HE IS STILL WORKING!*

MAKE IT PERSONAL

1.) The Greek word for "longsuffering" translates as *a strong and zealous passion under control."* What does this look like in action?

_____

_____

_____

_____

2.) What have you imagined "unity" to be in a family, a church, or an organization? After reading this chapter, has your view of "unity" changed or expanded?

_____

_____

_____

_____

3.) What unity principle(s) from Pastor Raymond Woodward spoke most to you? Explain.

_____

_____

_____

_____

4.) Starting today, how will you begin to cultivate longsuffering in your life?

_____

_____

_____

_____

5.) How will you begin to protect what God died for?

_____

_____

_____

_____

In an interview with Lee Strobel, Peter Kreeft concludes that the answer to suffering is not an answer at all. "It's the Answerer," says Kreeft. "It's Jesus Himself. It's not a bunch of words, it's **the** Word. It's not a tightly woven philosophical argument; it's a person.
The person.

The answer to suffering cannot just be an abstract idea, because this isn't an abstract issue; it's a personal issue. It requires a personal response. The answer must be someone, not just something, because the issue involves someone —
"God, where are you?"

— Lee Strobel,
The Case for Faith (Zondervan, 2000)

Final Thoughts

The Final Beatitude

*"**Blessed** are the poor in spirit, for theirs is the kingdom of heaven. **Blessed** are those who mourn, for they shall be comforted. **Blessed** are the meek, for they shall inherit the earth. **Blessed** are those who hunger and thirst for righteousness, for they shall be filled. **Blessed** are the merciful, for they shall obtain mercy. **Blessed** are the pure in heart, for they shall see God. **Blessed** are the peacemakers, for they shall be called sons of God. **Blessed** are those who are persecuted for righteousness' sake, for theirs is the kingdom of heaven. **Blessed** are you when they revile and persecute you, and say all kinds of evil against you falsely for My sake"* (Matthew 5:3-11).

His name was John. He was a miracle child. His father was a priest. His parents were old, well beyond

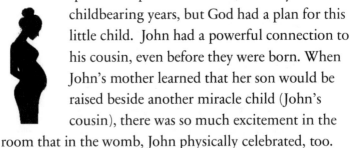

childbearing years, but God had a plan for this little child. John had a powerful connection to his cousin, even before they were born. When John's mother learned that her son would be raised beside another miracle child (John's cousin), there was so much excitement in the room that in the womb, John physically celebrated, too.

John the Baptist was a miracle child, conceived by elderly parents well beyond normal childbearing years. He was about six months older than Jesus (Luke 1:24-40), who

104

was miraculously conceived by the Holy Spirit (Matthew 1:18-21). Two children had been born, a strong, supernatural, and unshakable bond. John and Jesus grew up together, knew each other, and had a spiritual connection unlike any other. John grew and began to preach in the wilderness.

News of John's ministry spread, which drew many from their towns and homes into the wilderness to hear his preaching and to be baptized. He preached with conviction and with no filter. The opening verses of the Book of John speak clearly, *"There was a man sent from God, whose name was John.* **This man came for a witness, to bear witness of the Light, that all through him might believe.** **He was not that Light, but was sent to bear witness of that Light.** *That was the true Light which gives light to every man coming into the world"* (John 1:6-9).

John's anointing attracted crowds. He preached conviction, leading many to sincere repentance, and baptized many. His ministry was precise, powerful, and had been prophesied of roughly 400 years prior. *"Behold,* **I send My messenger, and he will prepare the way before Me.** *And the Lord, whom you seek, will suddenly come to His temple, even the Messenger of the covenant, in whom you delight. Behold, He is coming," says the Lord of hosts"* (Malachi 3:1). Interestingly, "Malachi" is a rendering of a Hebrew word meaning *"My messenger."*

Could you imagine the privilege of being the man who baptized Jesus, the Messiah? Imagine how humbling and awesome that would be. That kind of privilege was not random; these two men had a  profound connection. One the witness of Light, the other the Light of the world. One the baptizer of water, the other the Baptizer of Fire (Matthew 3:11).

When the time had come, Jesus began His earthly ministry. He called disciples to follow Him, and He went about preaching the gospel of the Kingdom (Matthew 4:23), doing many signs, wonders, and miracles. Later on, Jesus and His disciples visited the Judean countryside, where John was still preaching and baptizing. But John's ministry and influence began to fade, which became concerning to John's disciples.

*"So John's disciples came to him and said, "Rabbi, the man you met on the other side of the Jordan River, **the one you identified as the Messiah**, is also baptizing people. And everybody is going to him instead of coming to us." John replied, "No one can receive anything unless God gives it from heaven. **You yourselves know how plainly I told you, 'I am not the Messiah. I am only here to prepare the way for him.'** It is the bridegroom who marries the bride, and the bridegroom's friend is simply glad to stand with him and hear his vows. Therefore, I am filled with joy at his success. **He must become greater and greater, and I must become less and less**"* (John 3:26-30 NLT).

Before this, *"John saw Jesus coming toward him, and said, "Behold! The Lamb of God who takes away the sin of the world! This is He of whom I said, 'After me comes a Man who is preferred before me, for He was before me'"* (John 1:29-30).

"Again, the next day, John stood with two of his disciples. **And looking at Jesus as He walked, he said, "Behold the Lamb of God!"** *The two disciples heard him speak, and they followed Jesus"* (John 1:35-37).

On multiple occasions, John the Baptist made it very clear that he was not the Messiah but a witness, and he was to prepare the way for Him. John did not fail his calling. He was mighty in faith and unwavering in his convictions. John knew his purpose. He had the right spirit and attitude and did not glory in God's presence. Through God's power, John single-handedly prepared the way for the Messiah—the Lord of lords and King of kings!

But a miraculous birth, a prophesied destiny, revered at all levels of society (great and small), a powerful and anointed ministry, did NOT give John an exemption card for suffering and mistreatment. He didn't compromise. He stayed true to his purpose and calling. But circumstances

arose, and John found himself in a prison cell, barely escaping execution, at the hands of an evil King Herod (Luke 3:18-20, Matthew 14:1-5).

As time went by, there was no rescue, no liberation. Death was lurking around the corner each and every day in the solitary confinement of his cell. Rumors were swirling around the prison about how the king wanted to kill him without causing a stir among the people. John, the mighty trailblazer for the Messiah, now lay in his jail cell depressed, defeated, desperate, and doubting. John's disciples occasionally visited him in prison and told him how Jesus delivered, healed, raised the dead, and did amazing miracles everywhere He went.

In his mind, John thought, "Surely, Jesus can do something miraculous for ME. After all, I'm the one who prepared the way for Him. I'm His cousin. I have had a deep spiritual connection with Him since before we were born. Surely, He can and will deliver me out of this prison!" But days turned into weeks, weeks turned to months—without a word, without miraculous power, and without deliverance.

One day, *"John, calling two of his disciples to him, sent them to Jesus, saying, "Are You the Coming One, or do we look for another?" When the men had come to Him, they said, "John the Baptist has sent us to You, saying, 'Are You the Coming One, or do we look for another?'"* **And that very hour He cured many of infirmities, afflictions, and evil spirits; and to many blind He gave sight.** *Jesus answered and said to them, "Go and tell John the things you have seen and heard: that the blind see, the lame walk, the lepers are cleansed, the deaf hear, the dead are raised, the poor have the gospel preached to them..."* (Luke 7:19-22).

After seeing these supernatural signs and wonders and hearing Jesus' instructions, John's disciples turn and begin their journey back to the prison to tell John what they had seen and heard. I can imagine Jesus waiting for a moment as John's disciples began to make their departure. As they began to walk away, Jesus called out to them, "Tell John one last thing." John's disciples turned to face Jesus with anticipation and hope — *"And blessed is he who is not offended because of Me"* (Luke 7:23).

Why did Jesus not just answer John's disciples in this way? Why didn't Jesus come out with it and say, "Yes, I Am the Coming One!"? Why did Jesus instead perform miracles in their sight? Because when John sent word to Jesus, HE NEEDED AND WANTED A MIRACLE. John wanted to be delivered miraculously. John had faith to believe that Jesus could and would deliver Him from prison.

The response Jesus gave to John was a powerful one. It was as if Jesus was saying, "Yes, John, I have the power and ability to do miraculous things. I do have the power to deliver you, but I will not come to you and do it. Don't be

 offended, John, because you proceeded Me in life and in ministry to prepare the way. But you have one more task ahead of you. You will blaze one more trail, one for *My* execution at the hands of government officials.

You have done nothing wrong. You have lived pure and righteously. You have fulfilled your life's calling, yet you

will be executed. John, you must also prepare the way for my death. Because when the day comes, I WILL ALSO HAVE THE POWER TO SAVE MY OWN LIFE … BUT I WILL LAY IT DOWN. I will reign in my power for the salvation of others!" (John 10:18)

Friend, if John the Baptist, the forerunner of the Messiah, and Jesus our Messiah and King, had to endure suffering, sin, satan, and circumstances, so will we! God has the power to heal, deliver, resurrect, and save you from your trial and pain. He deserves all the praise and glory if He does so. *But what if He chooses NOT to deliver you?* What if the pain never goes away? What if this circumstance accompanies you to the end of your life's journey? *Will you be offended at God?*

"And blessed is he who is not offended because of Me" (Luke 7:23). It is the final beatitude. Jesus did not include it in His Sermon on the Mount. He saved the capstone of the beatitudes for His forerunner—the one who preceded Him in life, ministry, and death. *"Don't be offended in Me if I choose NOT to deliver you."*

"John, (put your name here _____) if I choose never to deliver you from this circumstance and you need to *suffer long* with it, understand that I will show you mercy through it all. My purpose will be revealed, and it is *much greater* than your need for deliverance and revenge. Though you may feel, at times, unable to bear it, I will give you the strength to endure. You will one day be saved (Matthew 24:13). Reign in your power to avenge, humble yourself, and get in partnership with My higher purpose and plan because endless joy, peace, and victory await us in eternity. *Don't be offended in Me. I am working all things together ... for good!"*

A preacher and his wife were on vacation, and as they walked down the busy city streets, they came upon a street painter. He was painting something exquisite on his canvas. A small crowd had gathered around him as he worked. After a few minutes, the artist had completed his work and turned to ask the crowd, "Who will give me $100.00 for this painting?" The people in the crowd looked at one another; whispers were heard, but no one stepped forward. The artist said, "Come on, folks, it's worth more than that. $100.00, any buyers?"

People began to walk away, and the painter became more upset. The preacher and his wife were turning to walk away when the painter yelled, "Fine if you all can't

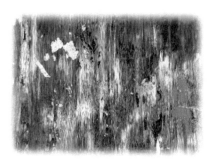

appreciate fine art, I'll show you what I will do with it." In an angry rage, he grabbed his palette and began throwing all sorts of dark paints over the canvas, virtually ruining his painting.

People stood in shock at what the painter had done. The preacher said to his wife, "This guy is an idiot. Let's go." His wife was about to turn and walk away when she saw the painter do something. "Hold on, dear..." she said. They watched as the artist started painting with all the haphazard colors on the canvas. They watched in amazement as a new and even more exquisite painting was created. The preacher and his wife bought that painting for $200.00.

The painting found a prime location in the preacher's office, just over his desk. Whenever he counseled someone whose life was going through pain, suffering, and

chaos, he would point to the painting and reminisce about what happened that day on the street. He would finish his story by saying, "God is the painter, and He is making a masterpiece. You may think God has ruined your life by allowing chaos and darkness to overwhelm you, and your original plans and expectations may be blacked out and never return, *but the Master Artist isn't done.* He can take all the chaos, dark colors, smears, and smudges and make an even more beautiful painting than what was there before. Don't be offended at God because He does something you can't understand. Don't quit. He is still painting a masterpiece."

Chaos may come. Pain may pierce our lives. Circumstances and offenses will come. But He is not done. Though we may need to endure with longsuffering, He has never, and will never, abandon you.

Tomatoes are designed to be consumed. That is their purpose. Tomatoes hold no value until they are cut open, sliced, mashed, peeled, and cooked— by the hands of another. Are you in the Master's hands? If He allows your life to be cut, smashed, sliced, and put through fiery trials, *don't be offended.* He will never allow you to go through anything He hasn't prepared, walked through, and overcome Himself. He is making something. He is doing something. He is working.

Jesus was sliced, smashed, and cut open, too. Though He suffered, He was victorious! Though Jesus bled from the wounds of sinful people (some even dressed in religious clothing), He was victorious! Though Jesus died and wasn't delivered from the cross, He was victorious! *Because there was a higher purpose for His suffering.* Though Jesus was buried in a borrowed tomb, *He arose victorious!*

My friend, victory is coming, even though you may be suffering right now. One of the most incredible things about being a child of the King is that even if we never experience victory over circumstances in our mortal life, *victory is still coming! Jesus is still coming! An endless eternity in Heaven is just over the horizon! A place He went to prepare for us! He is still working all things together for good, **even beyond this life!***

MAKE IT PERSONAL

1.) Can you relate to John the Baptist while he sat in prison, depressed and discouraged?

_____

_____

_____

_____

2.) Are you, or have you ever been, offended at God because He hasn't "come through" for you as you expected? Explain the offense towards God.

_____

_____

_____

_____

3.) Jesus never delivered John the Baptist from his prison cell, and John was later executed. What does this say to you? Why does God not choose to deliver at times?

_____

_____

_____

_____

4.) What have you learned while reading this final chapter?

_____

_____

_____

_____

5.) Are you willing to suffer long with your issues (even if God never chooses to deliver you)—without being offended at God? Can you still pursue a personal, intimate relationship with Him, regardless of your circumstances?

_____

_____

_____

_____

Endnotes

[1] Dictionary.com. (n.d.). Dictionary.com. https://www.dictionary.com/.

[2] *Oxford Learner's Dictionaries: Find definitions, translations, and grammar explanations at Oxford Learner's Dictionaries.* Oxford Learner's Dictionaries | Find definitions, translations, and grammar explanations at Oxford Learner's Dictionaries. (n.d.). http://www.oxfordlearnersdictionaries.com/.

[3] *English Dictionary, Translations & Thesaurus.* Cambridge Dictionary. (n.d.). https://dictionary.cambridge.org/.

[4] Wikimedia Foundation. (2020, December 24). *Nix v. Hedden.* Wikipedia. https://en.wikipedia.org/wiki/Nix_v._Hedden.

[5] NSTATE, L. L. C. (n.d.). Learn About the 50 States. State Symbols, 50 State Capitals, Flags, Maps, Geography, Facts, Songs, History, Famous People from NETSTATE.COM. http://www.netstate.com/.

[6] Lori Carrell, The Great American Sermon Survey (Mainstay Church Resources, 1999)

[7] National Institute of Mental Health, "U.S. Leading Categories of Diseases/Disorders," 2013

[8] Beck et al., 2014; Stewart, Ricci, Chee, Hahn, & Morganstein, 2003

[9] Bureau, U. S. C. (2020, July 19). *Calculating Migration Expectancy Using ACS Data.* The United States Census Bureau. https://www.census.gov/topics/population/migration/guidance/calculating-migration-expectancy.html.

[10] Alia Joy, Glorious Weakness: Discovering God in All We Lack, Baker Books, 2019. (Permission requested from author.)

[11] *Misdirected luggage.* Ministry127. (n.d.). Retrieved October 7, 2022, from https://ministry127.com/resources/illustration/misdirected-luggage

[12] Dictionary.com. (n.d.). Dictionary.com. https://www.dictionary.com/.

[13] www. sermoncentral.com

[14] www.illustrationexchange.com

[15] www. sermoncentral.com

[16] Story told in Stan Telchin, Betrayed (Chosen, 1981)

[17] Max Lucado, Facing Your Giants (W Publishing Group, 2006)

[18] Eric Miller, "Shock and Awe," *Books and Culture* (September – October 2006)

[19] Gary Preston, Character Forged from Conflict (Bethany, 1999)

Made in the USA
Columbia, SC
20 June 2024

36956003R00067